BEDSIDE
MANNERS

BEDSIDE MANNERS: GEORGE CLOONEY and ER

SAM KEENLEYSIDE

ECW PRESS

We acknowledge the support of the Canada Council
for the Arts for our publishing program.
This book has been published with the assistance
of grants from the Ontario Arts Council.

CANADIAN CATALOGUING IN PUBLICATION DATA

Keenleyside, Sam
Bedside manners: George Clooney and ER

Includes bibliographical references.
ISBN 1-55022-336-4

1. Clooney, George. 2. Television actors and actresses –
United States – Biography.
2. ER (Television program). I. Title.

PN2287.C546K43 1998 791.45 028 092 C979323967

Cover design by Guylaine Régimbald.
Front cover photo: WARNER BROS. / ARCHIVE PHOTOS
Back cover photo: Ron Wolfson / LONDON FEATURES

Imaging by ECW Type & Art, Oakville, Ontario.
Printed by Transcontinental Printing Inc., Sherbrooke, Québec.

Distributed in Canada by General Distribution Services,
30 Lesmill Road, Don Mills, Ontario M3B 2T6.

Distributed in the United States by Login Publishers Consortium,
1436 West Randolph Street, Chicago, Illinois, U.S.A. 60607.

Published by ECW PRESS,
2120 Queen Street East, Suite 200,
Toronto, Ontario M4E 1E2.

www.ecw.ca/press

PRINTED AND BOUND IN CANADA

For Lewis Robert "Hack" Wilson

AVG	G	AB	R	H	2B	3B	HR	RBI	BB	SO
.307	1348	4760	884	1461	266	67	244	1062	674	713

TABLE OF CONTENTS

ONCE UPON A CODPIECE

Joel Schumacher lets out a long sigh and settles into his comfortable first-class seat. He'd much rather be stretched out on his own leather sofa right now, but this won't be so bad. Soon enough he'll be handed a pillow and a much-needed drink by one of the leggy flight attendants prowling the airplane's aisles, and maybe, before too long, his mind will be able to settle down as successfully as his body has. But as hard as he tries to keep it locked safely in its cranial corral, his mind begins to wander. It's the mind of a film director, keenly observant and restlessly processing everything that passes before his eyes. Schumacher doesn't, as one might expect, break down everything he sees into a series of frames, snipping static moments right out of time and pasting them neatly into a virtual story-board. Instead, the images simply accumulate, one on top of the other, becoming part of the ever-evolving big picture that's constantly assembling itself in his head during his every waking moment.

Right now the big picture looks something like this: he's at the top of his game, having in the past two years directed the wildly popular screen adaptations of John

Grisham's best-selling novels *The Client* and *A Time to Kill*. There's talk of a Best Supporting Actor nomination for Samuel L. Jackson for the latter film, and the industry is still buzzing about Schumacher's prescient casting of a young hunk, Matthew McConaughey, whom many are calling the next Paul Newman. This kind of success is nothing new for Schumacher, who long ago staked his claim in Hollywood by directing the actions and soothing the egos of such hot young stars as Demi Moore, Kevin Bacon, Kiefer Sutherland, and Julia Roberts in movies like *St. Elmo's Fire*, *Dying Young*, and the cult hit *The Lost Boys*. He's also been credited with saving the floundering *Batman* film franchise by turning up the energy and unleashing the camp in the hip, visually spectacular *Batman Forever*.

But something keeps nibbling away at the margins of this picture, and Schumacher can't ignore it any longer. Val Kilmer, who replaced Michael Keaton in the title role in *Batman Forever*, won't be able to reprise the part because he'll be busy filming *The Saint* with Elizabeth Shue. Losing Kilmer complicates things a little bit, but it doesn't bother Schumacher too much; Kilmer did a solid enough job filling Batman's cowl, and was widely credited with breathing new life into the film series, but Schumacher knows that one actor — even one as talented as Kilmer — won't be allowed to make or break the franchise. Besides, Kilmer had, regrettably, lived up to his reputation as a temperamental perfectionist on the set, and Schumacher had his share of problems with the star until one day when he interrupted one of Kilmer's tirades and told him to get off his high horse and get his act together.

In fact, Schumacher is almost looking forward to the prospect of wiping the slate clean and starting anew with the next installment in the film series,

Batman and Robin. What with Kilmer's pouting and Tommy Lee Jones's condescending attitude toward nearly everyone on the set — he seemed to get into his character, supervillain Two-Face, just a little too thoroughly — Schumacher can't be blamed for wanting to clean house. "I'm really tired of defending overpaid, overprivileged actors," he tells *Cinescape*. "I don't know why we're protecting these people. Is it that we're supposed to be so afraid that they won't work with us again? I *pray* some of them don't work with me again." The idea of making changes doesn't

Clooney, coated in gore, in *From Dusk till Dawn*

J. RUDOLPH, DIMENSION / SHOOTING STAR

worry him at all. The real challenge, aside from finding somebody to take on a role that two Hollywood powerhouses have already made their own, will be convincing his bosses at Warner Bros. that the man he chooses will have enough box-office pull to pay dividends on their $100-million investment in the movie. He knows, despite his bravado, that he's set himself up for a harrowing next few months searching for a replacement. So much for relaxing and getting his mind off business.

It's now, in one of those coincidences that seem only to happen in Hollywood and Judith Krantz novels, that he looks down at the magazine that's been lying open in front of him all this time. He sees an advertisement for *From Dusk till Dawn*, the new blood-splattered creation of screenwriter Quentin Tarantino and director Robert Rodriguez. Schumacher hasn't seen the film, which has been getting lukewarm reviews at best from the stodgy critics whose voices ring loudest throughout the industry, and knows little about its star, George Clooney. Without even thinking, he begins to doodle on the ad. "I never get a chance to see television," he tells Oprah Winfrey later, "but I knew women were fainting and swooning, and my friends were telling me how great George Clooney was . . . and for some reason I took a black magic marker and I drew the bat cowl on him, and he looked *good*." Schumacher has seen enough pretty faces masquerading as actors, however, to know better than to get his hopes up. After all, he's never met Clooney, let alone seen him perform, and after his last *Batman* experience he wants above all to make sure there's good chemistry on his next set.

This seemingly harmless bit of doodling occupies his mind for the rest of his flight. He still can't shake this image the next day, or the next. A short while later, against his better judgment, he attends a screening of *From Dusk till Dawn*. Even amid the flying bullets, spurting blood, and morphing vampires, Clooney's screen presence is unmistakable. Schumacher knows it almost immediately: "He is a movie star." What he doesn't know, however, is whether Clooney, who has struggled to escape his image as little more than a pretty face in prime time and establish himself as a serious actor, will be interested in the part.

Schumacher needn't have worried. Like so many American boys in the '60s, Clooney grew up reading the comic-book adventures of the caped crusader and giggled his way, wide-eyed, through the campy action of the television series starring Adam West. In fact, he'd even worn the famous cowl before — though a decidedly less spectacular one than the Hollywood version — at Halloween parties as a kid. But Clooney couldn't possibly have known, or even have allowed himself to imagine, that he'd have the chance to portray his childhood hero on the big screen. Sure, his star had risen to impressive heights in Hollywood over the past year, but he wasn't so far removed from his days as a struggling actor that he could ignore the dangers of daring to believe his own hype. And although he can joke about it now, saying to Oprah with his usual wry smile that he had an ace up his sleeve in the form of some incriminating photographs of Schumacher with a farm animal, he was floored when Schumacher called him at his home and laid it all out for Clooney to see in his customary forthright manner: "Hey, do you want to star in one of the biggest movies of all time and one of the greatest film franchises in the world, [which] will give you a shot at a film career?" Not exactly a soft sell, but

Schumacher has never been one to employ under-statement in the service of landing big stars for his projects.

Trying to play it cool, Clooney nonchalantly re-plied, "Sure, Joel, sure," leaving it to Schumacher to approach the studio with the idea. But after hanging up and taking a moment to reassure himself there wasn't some other George Clooney that Schumacher had meant to call instead, he hit the speed dial and was on the phone with his cousin and childhood best buddy Miguel Ferrer, giggling like an idiot and rub-bing his face in disbelief over his sudden good fortune. "I called him because his hero growing up was Batman," Clooney reminisces for his *Cinescape* interviewer. "We used to sit around making plaster Batmans and goofy stuff like that as kids. I said to him, 'Guess what I'm going to do in September? I'm going to be in *Batman.*' Miguel is like, 'Oh, that's nice. What are you going to do, be a helper or something?' I said, 'No listen — I'm going to *be* Batman.'"

After killing himself laughing at Ferrer's manic, expletive-laden response to this good news, Clooney paused to take stock of the situation. This was, of course, his big break — though how much bigger it could really be than his current place at the center of ER, the highest-rated drama on network television, is difficult to imagine. Nevertheless, this was his oppor-tunity to become a bona fide movie star, to show that he had the stuff to propel a major motion picture, to play with the big boys. But it might also be his oppor-tunity to fall flat on his face. True to Schumacher's worries, Clooney had reservations about being the third Batman because he didn't want to be "the guy that screws up a very successful franchise. Especially one which will never be mine — Michael started it,

Val saved it. There's not a lot of places for me to go, except in the toilet."

But Clooney wasn't about to flush away the offer because of these misgivings. He hadn't worked so hard for so long just to give up such a potential career bonanza because he still had lingering doubts about whether he really deserved his fame and good fortune. In fact, as Clooney tells it, the decision came down to one basic notion: imagine how stupid he'd feel if he passed up this chance and never got another. "To me," he tells an *Us* interviewer matter-of-factly, "it's like playing *Let's Make a Deal* and not going for what's behind Curtain No. 3. Yes, it might end up being a rusty jalopy, but, hey, you know what? It may not be." But all of this was to some extent irrelevant now. He'd said yes to Schumacher's proposal and now could only sit back and see how it all played out.

Even though he'd agreed to take on the role, there was still much to do before Clooney would be fitted for his batsuit. Upon hearing Schumacher's appraisal of Clooney's viability not only as the next Batman, but also as a can't-miss leading man, Warner Bros. chairmen Bob Daly and Tery Semel set to work hammering out a deal that would augment Clooney's suddenly paltry $300,000-per-year contract with Warner's television arm, which produces ER. The good news was delivered by none other than Warner Bros. president of production Lorenzo di Bonaventura, who offered Clooney $5 million to star in the picture as part of a $25-million deal to do three films with the studio.

But financial considerations aside, there was also the matter of ER's production schedule, which doesn't leave much room for its stars to work on any other projects, let alone one as mind-bogglingly huge as *Batman and Robin*. One television executive, echoing industry sentiments in the *Detroit News*, asserted somewhat pettily, "If he's doing *Batman*, he ain't doing a full season, full-time, on ER. He'll do a scene here or there, [but] you don't take a hiatus during the television season." But these insiders underestimated Schumacher's resolve and Clooney's work ethic. Not only did he continue to put in 14-hour days on the set of ER from Monday through Thursday, but he also spent even longer days filming *Batman* on Fridays, Saturdays, and Sundays.

The work was more physically demanding than any he'd done before. And although there were days when it was nearly impossible for him to pull himself out of his nice warm bed to make the 6:00 A.M. call on the set of ER, he knew that he had to keep going, that he couldn't afford to lose his momentum and miss this chance now that it had finally presented itself. Like so many other things in his life, Clooney found himself able to boil down the angst of his bold career move into a simple home truth: "If at some point someone says to you, 'I'm gonna give you a shot at a film career — it doesn't mean it'll work, but you'll get a shot at it — but you're gonna have to work seven days for about a year and a half,' you do it," he said on *Prime Time Live*. And as draining as the work was — he'd never before had occasion to be bolted into a 45-pound rubber suit, no matter how much the tabloids wished that he had — it was exhilarating as well. On *Oprah*, Clooney summed up the arduous experience with his trademark common sense and humility: "The simple truth is you do it for a few months — you do it for six, seven months — and when you're finished you get to be Batman, so there isn't a whole lot to complain about."

Ferrer would visit him on the set, and the two would chat between takes, Clooney in full Batman regalia, trying desperately to cool himself down inside a suit rendered even more sweltering by the hot studio lights. Not that they conducted very many deep or wide-ranging discussions. Clooney described their conversations on *Prime Time Live* as consisting of little more than him asking, giddily, "Can you believe it?" and Ferrer shaking his head and replying, just as light-headedly, "No, I can't believe it."

The focal point of their disbelief isn't just the massive set they're occupying at the moment, though they might well be excused for gawking in slack-jawed awe at the brooding monoliths that surround them. Even Arnold Schwarzenegger, who will pack considerable box-office wallop into the film as the evil Mr. Freeze and who has been part of more than his share of Hollywood megaprojects, admits in *Cinescape*, "It stuns me how big this is. . . . The whole thing is just wild." Neither is their amazement caused by the presence of Schwarzenegger or any of the film's other stars, which include Chris O'Donnell as Robin, Alicia Silverstone as Batgirl, and Uma Thurman as the delectable villain Poison Ivy. For Clooney, all of this is somehow too unreal, too overwhelming, to believe. But the thing about the set that puzzles him the most is his own presence on it. He can't shake the feeling that he doesn't really belong here, that any moment now someone from the security staff is going to grab him by the collar and escort him from the premises for sneaking in while no one was looking, as has happened to a number of paparazzi who have been caught on the set.

But then he looks down to see that he doesn't have a collar to grab. He's slipped by them, safely shrouded in the batsuit. The suit does have its disadvantages, to be sure. As if the sheer weight of the thing weren't enough, there's also the small matter of being locked inside an inflexible rubber prison that can only be escaped with the help of technical support staff. Clooney winces as he describes for *Cinescape* what it's like to wear the oppressive outfit: "Have you ever walked around in rubber from head to toe all day long? I think they could call this the *Batman* diet. That's how hot the suit is. Buckets of sweat are pouring out of you. You feel light-headed. You can't hear a thing. Plus with that suit, it's not such a great idea to consume massive quantities of liquids, if you know what I mean." The costume's wearer has to adjust to having his ears covered in inch-thick rubber and having only a two-inch window on the world through the mask's eyeholes. Its one great advantage, however, is that if he can't see out, no one can see in, either. No one can invade his closely guarded personal space. No one can get a firm grip on the slippery man behind the mask. No one can see him long enough to ask the question he fears most: Does he have what it takes to make this work?

For a while, Clooney can evade the question, finding security in the batsuit — even when he's no longer wearing it — by deflecting discussion of himself, whenever possible, to the costume. But then Schumacher goes ahead and blows his cover by making an issue of the costume in his ongoing axe-grinding with Val Kilmer. He takes a cheap shot at the former Batman by telling the press, with malevolent glee, that Kilmer's old suit fits Clooney perfectly except for one small detail: its codpiece isn't large enough.

This feud is the last thing Clooney wants to get mixed up in, and he wonders aloud for an *Us* reporter why Schumacher and Kilmer can't just "worry about [their] own dicks and please leave my penis out of it."

Clooney and Chris O'Donnell as Batman and Robin

CHRISTINE LOSS, WARNER BROS. / AP/WIDE WORLD PHOTOS

That millions of filmgoers will now have their eyes glued to his crotch when he makes his big-screen appearance as Batman is the least of his worries. Schumacher's dig at Kilmer robs Clooney of his fleeting refuge, turning the costume into a trap instead of a haven. The batsuit is no longer the place he can hide from the questions about his ability to handle the role, but becomes the central focus of the question itself. He does his best to deflect the attention and controversy in a subtle, comical way by telling Oprah and Jay Leno that the size of his codpiece pales in comparison to co-star Chris O'Donnell's, but he can only slink out of the spotlight for so long. The squabble between Schumacher and Kilmer fades into silence, leaving Clooney to stand alone, suddenly vulnerable in his superhero's armor.

But the question remained: Could he really fill the caped crusader's codpiece?

ONE

BOY GEORGE

Kentucky's bluegrass country ranges lazily along the north-central portion of the state, dotting itself here and there with peaceful farming communities that snuggle themselves into, rather than interrupt, its lush green pastures and gently rolling hills. It's one of the most serenely beautiful stretches of land on the continent, a place whose bucolic charm might better be described as powerfully enchanting rather than simply delightful. This is especially true during the late-May blooming season of the lithe, willowy annual from which the state takes its famous nickname, when the grass turns to an ethereal bluish hue. There's something truly magical about this landscape, something about the otherworldly tint of the surrounding pastures that casts a spell on its observers, enticing them to surrender all cares and concerns to the nearly supernatural tranquillity of the scene.

Unfortunately, the spell only exercises its hold for a brief period. Its effect is cut short — literally — by the sounds of mowers, which trim the grass soon after its blooming, robbing the pastures of their entrancing blue undulations. What the farm equipment doesn't take care of is soon disposed of by the scores of roving livestock, which are more interested in feeding their bodies than feasting their eyes on the precious herbage. But these dull creatures instinctively understand something the casual observer is willing to apprehend only grudgingly. However disenchanting it may be for those who treasure it for its color alone, the true value of Kentucky bluegrass lies in its nutritive value. It is extraordinarily rich in calcium, and has for two centuries been the foundation upon which the state's prestigious breeding and rearing of horses has depended; American saddle horses, standardbreds, and the esteemed thoroughbreds lie at the center of Kentucky's lucrative equine industry. Sales, shows, and exhibitions of horses form the backbone of the business and take place all year long, while harness races, thoroughbred races, and steeplechases are held between April and November each year. The most famous of these, of course, is the Kentucky Derby, which has been run annually in Louisville, just outside bluegrass country, since 1875. One of the three jewels in thoroughbred racing's Triple Crown, the Derby is the moment at which Kentucky's rich country past and its profitable corporate present meet.

It was into this odd amalgamation of histories and values that bouncing baby boy George Clooney was born on May 6, 1961, in Lexington, Kentucky. Affectionately known by residents and tourists alike as the "Heart of the Bluegrass," this second largest of the state's cities blends the vim and vigor of a modern business center with the grace and charm of small-town life in the old South. Its temperament became an indelible part of Clooney's own, equipping him with the sophistication and savvy necessary to strike out on his own in Hollywood and the common sense and humility necessary to maintain his sense of himself once he got there.

Although it would be more than two decades before he set out for the West Coast in search of fame and fortune, Clooney got a taste of the entertainment industry at a very early age. His father, Nick, who had met mother Nina Warren while emceeing a beauty pageant in which she was first runner-up, was a local television celebrity who'd dreamed since early childhood of being part of the most powerful entertainment vehicle of his generation: broadcast radio. Nick and his sisters, including renowned torch singer Rosemary, would gather around the radio every night in their hometown of Maysville, Kentucky, and imagine their own voices ringing out through the open air. Their home life was not particularly strict, but it was nonetheless confining. Both parents had to work to make ends meet — his mother in a clothing store and his father by painting houses, a job made thankless by the heavy fumes of oil-based paints that robbed him of his energy, and even his appetite, by the time he got home after his long day on the job.

The economic constraints placed on the family were, however, never allowed to interfere with the children's aspirations. Father and mother instilled the work ethic and furnished the moral support, and radio provided the dream. Limited only by the ranges of their imaginations, the young Clooney children envisioned the empty space through which the radio waves traveled and wondered aloud how truly liberating it might be to roam through that space themselves. Sisters Rosemary and Betty longed to entertain like the silky-voiced divas of radio's golden age. For his part, Nick identified with the proper intonations of the shows' hosts and radio newsmen. There he'd be, at seven and eight years old, rolling up a newspaper and pretending it was a microphone as he mimicked the rhythms and inflections of his favorite broadcasters' polished voices.

Although Nick and his sisters refused to believe for even a moment that they wouldn't somehow make it on the air, none of them really knew how to go about doing so. It was easy enough to dream the dream, but turning it into a reality — and, just as importantly, into a steadily paying job — was another thing altogether.

Clooney, with dad Nick

LAURA D. LUONGO / SHOOTING STAR

They had no formal training in the industry and, even worse, no connections. Fortunately, they did have gifts of their own. In Rosemary's and Betty's case, it was the gift of a golden voice. The sisters did local singing tours, which eventually garnered them time on the air and led to stardom for Rosemary. Nick, though, was no crooner. He realized before long that he'd have to get by on gumption alone. So one afternoon, when he was only 16 years old, he accepted the challenge posed to him by some friends and strutted into a local radio station to apply for work.

He got the job and before long became a familiar voice on WFTM, "The Golden Buckle of the Tobacco Belt." Still, as much as he loved the work and the people, part of him wanted to move on. He had an insatiable desire to be heard by more listeners, and in different places, so he enlisted in the U.S. Army and travelled overseas to work for the much-respected Armed Forces Radio Network. Here he gained invaluable broadcast experience and the sense that his voice was an important part of something far larger than he'd ever imagined as a child. He wasn't just speaking into a microphone, he was *communicating* with the world.

On returning home to Kentucky in 1955, he entered the television business, still searching for the most effective way to reach an audience he couldn't even see. He hosted a variety show on the local network affiliate, and then moved to a succession of slightly larger jobs in slightly larger towns. He'd stay in one place, he recalls for the *Columbus Dispatch*, until he felt he was "good enough to go somewhere else." Before long he was toting his young family — which included George and daughter Ada — along with him from city to city, gig to gig, throughout Kentucky and neighboring Ohio.

It was, to say the least, an unsettled childhood for
young George. In eight years of schooling, he attended
five different schools, and he lived in everything from
a modest bungalow to one of the ornate Georgian
manors, with their ivy-covered walls and solid white
doors, which can still be found in Lexington's older
neighborhoods. Whereas his father's childhood had
been spent within a strictly circumscribed geographi-
cal and economic compass, George's was positively
nomadic. "Life at our house was a lot different than
many others'," George tells his *Biography* interviewer,
"because Pop had a different job every year or every
week. We'd live in a mansion, then a very modest
house. We always had a fairly comfortable life, but
there was nothing guaranteed."

Luckily, what the Clooney family lacked in geo-
graphical stability it more than made up for in warmth
and caring. George and his sister were never allowed
to forget the importance of family, and were reminded
constantly that the sacrifices they made for their
father's career were really only investments in a dream,
and that one day, when they began to follow dreams
of their own, those investments would reap huge dividends. Kentucky's state motto became the Clooney
family's own: "United we stand, divided we fall."

It was during these years that George took his first
tentative steps into the limelight of local television,
making brief appearances on his father's morning
show whenever the opportunity presented itself. He
had, long before ever setting foot on a soundstage or
mugging for a camera, always been an entertainer. He
reveled in his status as class clown and would clamor
to be the center of attention at family reunions — no
easy task given some of the talent that surrounded
him at these occasions. His father remembers these

reunions as being more than just a chance to reaffirm family ties. They were, in a way, cutthroat talent contests at which, Nick tells *People* magazine, "everyone had his schtick. George determined that his was going to be better than anyone else's — and by golly it was." Although no one in the family really cared to wager on what George would end up doing with his life — he seemed too interested in living for the moment for anyone to imagine that he was thinking about his future just yet — they all agreed that, for all his goofiness, George had *something* that set him apart from others.

Unlike many children, he had the chance to groom that something from an early age. His beginnings were inauspicious, to be sure, though they sure beat starting out in the role of the tree in the school play. At the age of seven, he, along with his older sister, would be drafted to appear on his father's live variety show. It was decidedly cornball stuff, but Clooney can't help but speak of those days with an affectionate smirk on his face. "If it was Easter," he tells *Tribute*, "I'd put on a rabbit suit and be the Easter bunny. If it was St. Patrick's Day, I got a leprechaun outfit and a cigar, and my dad would interview me." It's hard to picture him today, decked out in a glittering green top hat and plaid knickers, and it was probably experiences such as this that gave him his present ability to deadpan his way through almost any conversation, no matter how painfully funny or purely bizarre it might be.

For a while, in fact, his father was convinced beyond a shadow of a doubt that George would pursue a career as a stand-up comedian, but he's hardly surprised now that Clooney has become a so-called "serious actor" instead. Even at a young age, Nick tells the *Columbus*

Dispatch, George had "an amazing ability to connect with the camera." As he got older, George began to act in more elaborate skits on his father's shows, but he also showed an aptitude for the less glamorous side of show business life. He did everything from holding cue cards to organizing properties behind the scenes, and he was a reliable worker. Sure, he was apt to horse around at regular intervals, but once the red light went on in the studio — this was, after all, live television — he could be counted on to do as he had been asked.

It seemed for a time, tragically, that Clooney would be relegated to backstage life forever. Just when his family seemed to be more settled than they had been in years — they lived in a beautiful Victorian house in Augusta, Kentucky, from which Nick would drive each morning to nearby Cincinnati to work on his most successful program to date — things fell apart. It began innocently enough one weekend when George was a 15-year-old high school student. He had stayed up late Saturday night watching television, mesmerized by Gary Cooper's magnificent performance as Lou Gehrig in *The Pride of the Yankees*. George was not just the class clown, he was also the class athlete, and he saw in Gehrig an incredible combination of athleticism and humanity. He'd have given anything to be just like the Iron Horse.

The next morning, while sitting in church, his attention began to drift from the day's sermon, and he found himself daydreaming about what it might be like to be a major-league baseball player or, better yet, a player as wonderful as Gehrig. What must it be like to have the world in the palm of your hand? To be the hero of millions of adoring fans? To have everything that life had to offer and then some? It was about this time that a strange sensation began to overtake him. The left side of his face started to tingle oddly, as if it had fallen asleep. His tongue suddenly felt like a warm chunk of lead in his mouth. What was happening to him?

He did his best to ignore these strange feelings, more irritated that they had interrupted his daydreams than concerned that they might be an indication of something more serious. But then, while eating lunch with his family, he noticed that he couldn't feel the area around his left eye at all. He attempted to close the eye, all the while trying not to attract the attention of the rest of the people at the table, and found that he couldn't. Worse still, when he tried inconspicuously to take a swig from his glass, milk poured from his rubbery lips and dribbled down the side of his face. It dawned upon him in a flash of irony: he had Lou Gehrig's disease. This was it. His life was over. Instead of living the dream of a professional sports career like Gehrig's, all he'd been granted was the nightmare of a slow and debilitating death. This sudden realization was devastating.

It was also, as things turned out, quite incorrect. He didn't have Lou Gehrig's disease — or amyotrophic lateral sclerosis, as it is known in medical circles — at all. What he did have was Bell's palsy, a disfiguring paralysis of one facial hemisphere that strikes approximately 1 in 10,000 people without warning. Although the affliction usually runs its course in a matter of weeks or months, its effects can last a lifetime. Sometimes — as in the case of Canadian prime minister Jean Chrétien, another famous casualty of the disorder — the facial muscles never regain their original strength and elasticity, leaving the victim with drooping lips and eyelids or a permanent sneer. "I was sobbing, just a wreck," Clooney confesses to an *Us* reporter. And who can blame him? Granted, it wasn't the death

sentence he had originally feared, but the prospect of
spending an indeterminate period of his adolescence
— and quite possibly his entire life — with a distorted
face must surely be the next worse thing a 15-year-old
boy can imagine.

Luckily, perhaps due to the fact that — what with
all his mugging for friends and family — his face was
remarkably elastic to begin with, it did, within a year's
time, regain its original form. Few people are likely to
confuse George Clooney with Jean Chrétien anytime
soon. Still, the disease very nearly ruined his life. That
year of high school was the most horrible time of
Clooney's adolescence. Even more difficult to bear
than his classmates' stares was their polite willingness
to look away when he approached. He was in limbo
and found it impossible to believe this was happening
to him. Were it not for his sense of humor, he probably would have emerged from the experience with
emotional scars far more serious than any cosmetic
damage the affliction could ever render. He somehow managed to laugh at himself over those long 12
months, working his disfigurement into his comic
schtick in order to hide his anxiety.

Two years later, having recovered fully from the
effects of the temporary facial paralysis, he was confi-
dent enough in his appearance to don a mauve tuxedo
(yes, these were the '70s) and escort one of the pretti-
est girls in town, a college freshman named Laura
Laycock, to the 1978 Augusta High School prom.
Although the tux did clash with his mode of trans-
portation that evening — he had borrowed his dad's
ultracool red-and-white Corvette for the occasion —
Clooney pulled off his comeback without a hitch.
He spent the night dancing, partying, and, in a sure
sign that he was still his same old self despite his

frightening experience, playing the fool. His date remembers him doing hilarious imitations of his friends and mercilessly teasing everyone he laid his eyes on. "It was just part of George goofing around," she reports on *People* on-line.

But the time for goofing around was drawing perilously short. High school was nearly over, and there were decisions — important decisions — to be made. It was time for him to decide what he was going to do with his life. It was time for him to move beyond the boy's life and into the man's. It was time for him to get serious.

HARD AT WORK AND HARD AT PLAY

Clooney shouldered the burden of having to prove he could take life seriously by enrolling in Northern Kentucky University, where he got right down to some serious drinking. He sums up his college days for *Biography* in a single sentence: "I partied a lot, got drunk a lot." He also got high a lot, tripping out on the acid and magic mushrooms that were so readily available on campus. Trouble was, he didn't study a lot. It would be too simplistic to say that college life just wasn't for him. In fact, he loved college life. Hanging with the boys, whooping it up at wild parties, flirting (and more) with plenty of attractive women — what full-blooded American young man wouldn't love it? As for schoolwork . . . well, he could always catch up on that. Or so he thought.

It's not easy to attend early-morning classes on the best of days, but it's even harder to do when you've spent the entire weekend beforehand in one of three states of consciousness: drunk, asleep, or hungover. Clooney wasn't the first guy to blow off his university courses in favor of a booming social life, and he certainly won't be the last. He was, however, the first son of Nick Clooney to do so, and Pop, as George calls him, was none too pleased. If there was one thing Nick had tried to instill in his son, it was respect for the importance of hard work, a respect he had learned over his years of diligent labor in the broadcasting field. It was George's willingness to toss this lesson aside so cavalierly, and not just his bad grades, that made his father see red. Part of Nick wanted to grab his son by the collar and give him a good, hard shake. Couldn't he see that he was throwing his life away? Didn't he know that nothing would ever be handed to him on a silver platter?

But something held Nick back. It wasn't just his calm, amiable nature; he could be firm — even strict — when necessary. He hadn't come as far as he had on his own without being able to put his foot down with an authority that could be imposing and even a little scary. But he knew two things for certain. First, George would only be convinced of the importance of hard work if he found his way to it himself. For all his charm and good humor, he was a stubborn kid, and no one was going to tell him what to do. He'd have to choose the path toward success for himself, if he wanted to choose at all. Second, Nick just had a feeling in his gut that this kid couldn't miss, that his talent would eventually win out over his childishness and pull him toward success no matter how hard he tried to screw things up.

After three years at university, George finally called it quits. The truth was, he'd never really had any intention of going to college at all. His first love was baseball, and he had been bound and determined that he was going to play in the major leagues — if possible, for his beloved Cincinnati Reds. He knew better than to dream of having a career like Lou Gehrig's; the last time he'd wished for this he'd got into a lot of trouble, and he wasn't nearly the hitter that Gehrig had been. But he truly believed that, if given a chance, he could catch somebody's eye. He was a good enough ballplayer, and how hard could it possibly be? Throw the ball, catch the ball, hit the ball, run. He could do it. He was sure he could.

The talent scouts were less sure. After completing high school, he tried out twice for the Cincinnati Reds, and didn't do too badly at all. Hitting a well-thrown baseball is one of the hardest things to do in sports. When perfect contact between round ball and curved bat is made, the hitting area is just a touch smaller than a dime. Make contact even a scant millimeter beyond this circumference and you've got a short pop-up or a weak grounder. But Clooney was right on the money, and did an impressive job with the bat. He was also steady in the outfield, getting a good jump on the ball by using his knack for anticipating where a hitter was going. Even though he didn't have blazing speed, he managed to cover a lot of ground in centerfield because of his instincts for the game.

Unfortunately, his lack of speed eventually did him in. It also didn't help that he didn't have a great throwing arm — not a huge concern if you're a first baseman, but absolutely crucial if you're going to patrol the outfield. What's more, Cincinnati was still a powerhouse team at the time, having just come off back-to-back World Series wins in 1975 and 1976 with its Big Red Machine. How could he honestly have expected to break into a lineup that featured such baseball luminaries as Johnny Bench, Joe Morgan, Dave Parker, and Tony Perez? It was after his second failed tryout that he had reluctantly decided to enroll at Northern Kentucky University, doing so only because he couldn't think of anything better to do.

Now, after three fun-filled years, he was leaving school. Considering that he still hadn't completed enough courses to be designated a sophomore, the school's administrators weren't exactly begging him to stay. He'd been looking for a way out almost from the moment he'd set foot on the campus, and was finally presented with one when he got a call from his cousin, Miguel Ferrer. Miguel was back in Lexington, shooting a low-budget film with his father, José Ferrer. The elder Ferrer, husband of George's aunt Rosemary, was a star in his own right. He'd appeared in numerous Hollywood projects, including such legendary films as *The Greatest Story Ever Told* and *The Caine Mutiny*, but often involved himself in smaller works if he liked the script or the people involved.

Clooney landed a small part in the film, and managed that only because Miguel and José could hardly say no to a member of the family. The job didn't pay much, and the movie, it turned out, was too dreadful to be released. But Clooney was unperturbed. In fact, he was elated. He'd actually been paid to perform for the first time in his life and, better yet, found that he really liked doing it. That he wasn't particularly good at it didn't really matter to him right now: "I was truly seduced by acting," he told *Biography*. Just like that, he decided that he should pack up his bags and head for Hollywood.

His father thought he was crazy. A failed actor himself — he'd taken a few futile stabs at screen acting before coming to the conclusion that he didn't have the requisite talent — he let his son know what he thought of the idea in no uncertain terms: "I told him it was the dumbest thing I ever heard of," he told *Biography*. What did George know about acting, much less Hollywood? And apart from the question of how George would support himself when, and if, he got there, how was he going to fund the cross-country trip to Hollywood? Nick made it clear that, after the NKU fiasco, there was no way he was going to shell out the dough for George's latest escapade. He could depend upon his family for moral support, but nothing more. He was on his own.

Nick should have known that, no matter how much he intended his words to dissuade his son from this harebrained scheme, everything he said was likely only to convince George to work as hard as he could to make his dream come true. Hadn't he said all along that George would only put his nose to the grindstone when he decided for himself that there was something worth working toward? True to his father's prediction, but contrary to his wishes, George began to work to put together enough money to finance a move to Hollywood. He made a little money selling women's shoes at McAlpine's in Kentucky, but nothing to speak of. Besides, he really wasn't cut out for that particular line of work. He was a hit with the clientele, to be sure. With his charm, he had the blue-haired ladies who frequented the department store in the palm of his hand. Unfortunately, his job demanded that he also have their feet in the palm of his hand, and Clooney didn't have the stomach for it.

He could get past the fact that the women he met were inveterate liars about their shoe sizes, always demanding that he try to cram their feet into shoes one or two sizes too small for them. That part of the job just required patience and the willingness to do what he could to help some poor woman's foot defy the laws of physics. What really killed him were the feet themselves, the gnarled, misshapen, fungus-infested hooves that he'd have to pretend belonged to a beautiful Cinderella rather than one of her wicked stepsisters. Among the most horrifying of his customers were an 80-year-old woman with a hammertoe and a number of women who'd had a toe cut off so that they could wiggle their feet into a pair of pumps. It was, he tells Oprah, "a horrible, horrible, horrible job to do."

Many people would use precisely the same words to describe tobacco cutting, but Clooney quit his job at McAlpine's and headed for Lexington's tobacco fields nevertheless. Before the Civil War, most of the farmers in bluegrass country grew hemp, a tough, fibrous herb cultivated for use in cloth as cordage. (Clooney had, of course, become quite familiar with hemp in its more common form — marijuana — during his college days, but that's another matter altogether.) But two factors had put an end to the booming hemp industry in the area. The first of these was the advent of steam power, which made the use of hemp-based rope and rigging on ships nearly obsolete. The second was the Civil War itself. The area's farmers couldn't help but notice the number of soldiers who would take a moment to roll themselves a cigarette as they moved about the fields, and decided that it might be wise to take advantage of the market for tobacco. Before long, the vast majority of Lexington hemp farmers had converted their crops to tobacco, so that today, nearly 140 years later, Lexington is one of the most important tobacco centers in the world, supplying all of the dark, air-cured tobacco used for chewing and nearly 90 percent of the leaf tobacco used for snuff on the global market.

So there Clooney found himself, hacking away at tobacco plants as part of a cutting crew made up of a handful of guys his age, some down-on-their-luck older men, and a number of migrant workers from as far away as California. It was grueling work, and he'd come home at night exhausted, with blisters on his blisters from swinging the heavy blade and sore muscles in his arms, back, and shoulders from hoisting bundles of tobacco into large piles for baling. But Clooney liked it, or at least didn't completely hate it. It was, in a strange way, a very life-affirming way to make a living. He'd spend the day having to depend on nothing other than his own muscles, which hardened and fit more closely to his skeleton than they had in his slightly heavier days as a terminal freshman. He savored the company of the good old boys who'd tell dirty jokes and off-color stories about their own young lives while chewing, it seemed, more tobacco than they ever cut. Besides, anything was better than selling shoes for a living.

When he had finally made enough money in the tobacco fields, Clooney, now 21, sank part of his fortune into an old jalopy — a 1976 Monte Carlo — and, with $300 in his pocket and a promise from Aunt Rosemary that he could stay with her until he got on his feet, set out for Hollywood. As romantic as it might be to say that the young man sped off to meet his destiny with nary a care in the world, the plain truth is that he limped out of town in his maroon bucket of bolts, worried sick that the damn thing would break down. The Danger Car, as he called it, couldn't travel faster than 50 miles per hour, but eventually it got him there. Now all he had to do was figure out what he was going to do with himself now that he'd arrived.

He spent a year in his aunt's Hollywood home,

earning his keep by doing odd jobs around the house and chauffering her and her friends around town. Rosemary was definitely not a demanding boss, but she made sure to get on his case just enough to let him feel that he wasn't taking advantage of the situation. He was, in her affectionately gruff estimation, "an okay kid," and she did what she could to look out for him and help him out. Clooney doesn't speak much of those days, but he has told the gem of a tale about the summer he drove Rosemary and fellow performers Kaye Ballard, Helen O'Connell, and Martha Raye on their three-state 4 Girls 4 Tour. As George tells the story to *Us* magazine, the car was rocketing down the interstate when Clooney, at the wheel, got a request from the back seat to pull over to the side of the road. He didn't much want to stop — after having inched his way across the country in his Monte Carlo, it felt wonderful to go over the speed limit — but his passenger was insistent. He slowed the car and pulled fully onto the shoulder of the road. Out got Martha Raye, who proceeded to relieve herself quite noisily just to the side of the car's rear passenger-side fender. Whether it was to quell her nephew's embarrassment or just to take an easy shot at Raye, Rosemary suddenly cracked from the back seat, "Don't turn around, George. You'll learn too much about the aging process." Needless to say, George didn't turn around. He'd already learned as much as he cared to from his days selling shoes, and he knew that anything he might see back there would be a lot more unsettling than that ugly old hammertoe back at McAlpine's.

As adventurous as his early days in Hollywood were, he did find himself wondering, occasionally, if he'd made the right decision. Maybe his father was right. Maybe it would have been wiser to pursue a more sensible occupation back in Kentucky or Ohio, where he'd have plenty of connections through his old man. A steady job, a good salary, a place of his own . . . yes, it might be nice. Then again, he knew there would be constant expectations from people back home that he live up to Nick's example, and he wasn't sure he could, or even that he wanted to try. Furthermore, he'd always had the sense that, no matter how fulfilled his father seemed in his successful news career, there was a part of Nick that regretted not having made any serious attempt to become an actor himself. Now, George has told a GQ interviewer, he believes that "there's a part of [Pop] that goes, *I wonder*. For whatever reasons, he didn't take the chance to do it, and I think he regrets that."

Back then, as he pondered his circumstances and how they might lead him to a successful future as an actor, he came to the conclusion that he'd rather try his damnedest and fail than live the rest of his life wondering what might have been. If he was going to have regrets, it wouldn't be because he hadn't at least tried. If he failed, he failed. So be it. But for now he was simply going to work harder than he ever had in his life to make his dream come true.

THREE

GEORGE IN THE JUNGLE

Now that George had decided to commit himself to making it big in Hollywood, he needed a plan of action. First he swore that no matter how discouraged he might become, he wouldn't go to Rosemary and ask her if she could use her pull in Tinseltown to get him into auditions through the back door. He wanted desperately to prove that he could make it on his own. What's more, he already felt that he was putting his aunt out by staying in her home, and he had inherited far too much of his father's pride to allow himself to become a full-blown charity case. As much as he appreciated Rosemary's hospitality, he knew deep down that he had to make a break as soon as he could. He was too independent a person to allow himself to feel beholden to others for too long, no matter how much he loved or respected them.

Then again, being independent didn't mean he was going to be downright stupid. For the time being, living with his aunt had one great advantage that convinced him to stay put: if he lived with her, doing small jobs for her to cover room and board, he wouldn't have to worry about finding steady employment to pay his own rent. This would give him time to scour the city for acting jobs, and might even allow him the luxury of taking some nonpaying gigs that would be far more valuable for the experience they could provide him with than for the paycheck he would be passing up. Rosemary said proudly on the *Late Late Show* that George "went out for *everything*. He went out for every audition that he could get into. He did all of the showcases, all the things on Melrose in the little theaters for no money, and he worked *hard*. He worked very, very hard."

The only trouble was that he had nothing to show for it other than an ever-increasing pile of soiled and sweaty T-shirts whose collars had been ruined by the cheap pancake makeup he'd wear each night as he trod the wobbly boards of those poorly lit theaters. He spent the bulk of that year, 1982, with his ear to the ground, listening closely for even the faintest rumblings of yet another audition. When he heard the telltale signs of the latest cattle call, he'd be right there with the dozens of other eager young wannabes, praying that this audition would end with him dining on a celebratory steak dinner rather than being left, once again, on the cold slaughterhouse floor. He did get some callbacks, during which the shows' casting staffs, having thought they'd seen something in him when he did his original auditions, never seemed able to see it a second time. It wasn't the constant rejection that discouraged Clooney so much as his unswerving belief that he really was better than some of the lunkheads who ended up with parts. What did they have that he didn't?

One day it dawned on him that he'd been thinking too much about competing with the other actors, and not concentrating hard enough on what he had to do when he got in the room to audition. It was like coming to bat in the ninth inning of a close ball game and hoping he'd be able to draw a walk rather than taking his cuts and trying to win the whole damn thing with a single swing of the bat. What he'd thought all along was confidence in himself had turned out to be nothing more than hope that the other guy would screw up and leave him with the part. He'd been cocky up to now, he told *Prime Time Live*, joking with false bravado that people who would approach him saying "Isn't it awful being known as Nick Clooney's son?" would soon be asking Nick "Aren't you George Clooney's father?" But his attitude was a put-on, a pose he struck to avoid being asked — or having to ask himself — whether he truly had the aplomb to seize the moment and make it his own.

Luckily, Clooney had worked through a similar confidence problem in his baseball days, and it was his ability to draw on his athletic experience that finally inspired him to give himself a kick in the pants. "When I used to play baseball," Clooney remembers, "there was a time when I couldn't hit to save my life. Then one day I came to the park, and instead of thinking, *I wonder whether I'm going to get a hit today*, I said, *I wonder which field I'm going to get a hit to today.* And it worked." What he needed to do now, he determined, was apply the same cause-and-effect logic to his present situation. "I decided to go in and read for parts not like *I hope, I hope, I hope I get the part*, but like I was the best thing that ever happened to them," he tells GQ. "I started acting like the best actor they'd ever seen. And I started getting parts." Not great parts, mind you, but parts nonetheless. Clooney had been in the trenches long enough to see that one thing often led to another in Hollywood, and he wasn't about to

Clooney and Elliott Gould on the short-lived sitcom E/R

SHOOTING STAR

turn down any part, no matter how small, that had even the slightest potential of leading to something else or giving him an in at the next audition.

One of his first big breaks, if it can be called that, was in 1984, when he landed a role on a mercifully short-lived CBS sitcom called, coincidentally enough, *E/R*. It's tempting, nearly 15 years later, to say that getting this part was an omen of Clooney's eventual success on the similarly named NBC drama. But the truth is that, as painfully bad as it was, the CBS show could be more accurately described as a harbinger of death. It certainly did its part in killing the career of the show's star, Elliott Gould. Before *E/R*, Gould had starred in *Capricorn One* and Robert Altman's *The Long Goodbye* and *M*A*S*H*, which inspired the long-running sitcom in which Alan Alda took over the reins as Hawkeye Pierce. After *E/R*, Gould was reduced to punching the clock on the sets of such legendary pieces of work as *Dangerous Love* and *Wet and Wild*

Summer, an unwatchable, lewd takeoff on the Frankie Avalon and Annette Funicello beach movies of the '60s. By comparison, his work on *The Muppets Take Manhattan* seems positively brilliant.

Luckily, Clooney didn't really have a career to ruin at this point. He plodded through his paces on the show as a dim-witted intern named Ace, knowing all the while that this was really bad work, but hoping like hell it couldn't get any worse. It was during this time, perhaps as a way of trying to fit into the Hollywood scene, that he began to renew his image as a party animal, which he had pretty much shelved since his college days. He was back to living large, attending all the parties he could and usually finding himself in a strange woman's bed the next morning, wondering not only how he had got there, but also how best to beat a hasty retreat without seeming like too much of a jerk. He'd also be battling a wicked hangover and the peculiar fuzzy-headedness that afflicts a person who has done cocaine the night before.

Despite his naughty behavior, however, Clooney never got close to the point of being a candidate for the Betty Ford Clinic. He wasn't the type to constantly have the spoon at his nose for a refreshing hit of blow, and would only take an occasional snort of coke to give himself a quick boost of energy at parties. Clooney tells GQ that the habit, if it could even be called that, only lasted a couple of years because he found that the momentary buzz of energy it provided wasn't worth the post-rush depression that would set in. Besides, he was much more comfortable in an alcohol-induced stupor than a cocaine-induced one, and he didn't much like ingesting anything that tended to inhibit him from being the life of the party. A few good, stiff drinks would give him a mild adrenalin

rush that propelled him to the center of attention at
any party, but the coke only slowed him down and
made him paranoid. After finding himself spending
too much time at parties, nodding in dopey agreement
with some inane conversation, he decided he'd had
enough of that particular form of recreation.

It took even less time for CBS to decide that it had
had enough of *E/R*. It was almost a relief when the
show was finally yanked off the air, though it did mean
that George would have to start pounding the pave-
ment once again. This time, however, it was much less
daunting. Armed with his newfound self-confidence
and a resume that now actually included a bona fide
television credit, he strutted into his auditions with
an almost cocksure manner. There was nothing non-
chalant about his approach — this was, after all, a man
who once burst into the office of a vice-president at
ABC and, with the help of four friends, set up a bunk
bed right on the spot and began to deliver lines from
Brighton Beach Memoirs — but he knew that if he could
only project it effectively, his confidence in himself
would spread around the room, and before long the
powers-that-be would have confidence in him too.

His strategy worked. Over the next couple of years,
he impressed enough people in enough auditions to
be given roles on eight different television pilots, but
he was caught in an inescapable good-news/bad-news
situation. The good news was that he appeared in
eight pilots. The bad news was that appearing in that
many pilots over that short a span of time meant that
none of them was picked up by the networks. Looking
back on them now, Clooney is almost wistful when he
thinks of some of the shows he worked on. It's with
a certain measure of pride that he can say to *Prime
Time Live*, "I've done a lot of very bad television, and

I've been *very bad* in a lot of bad television." If there was a silver lining here, it was that he got paid regardless of whether the pilots got off the ground or not. For a while he was, as his Aunt Rosemary called him on the *Late Late Show*, "the best-paid unknown actor in town." This didn't exactly mean that he was rolling in dough, but his income did enable him to move out of Rosemary's house and get a place of his own — although he did, after running low on cash, spend eight months sleeping in the closet of a friend named Tom Matthews, who was less amazed at the fact that Clooney would be willing to sleep in a closet than at the number of women he somehow convinced to spend the night with him there.

Before long he was out of the closet and on his feet. In 1986, at the age of 25, he joined the cast of *The Facts of Life*, a sitcom that had lost touch with its viewership and seemed to sink lower in the ratings the older its

Clooney learns about *The Facts of Life*
NBC / KOBAL

teenage stars became. There was only so much teen-age angst to be exploited by Mrs. Garrett and the girls, apparently, so Clooney was brought on in the role of a carpenter who'd spent the last few years install-ing hot tubs in Kuwaiti homes. Of course, he didn't much look like a carpenter, but that hardly mattered. Not the suave leading man that he is today, Clooney played the part with just enough of his natural boyish cuteness to elicit mild shrieks from the adoring teeny-boppers at home without threatening those girls' mothers with even the smallest hint of testosterone. In another segment of the industry, the show's scenario might give rise to a much different kind of production. An attractive young man frequents an establishment called Edna's Edibles, which houses a handful of nubile sorority girls? Sounds like an adult film in the making. But in the capable hands of network television, it made for wholesome cornball comedy, just the kind of family-values viewing that even Dan Quayle could love.

Clooney also managed to get some film work dur-ing this time, though it wasn't of the sort that attracts much notice come Oscars time. He got bit parts in such turkeys as *Return to Horror High*, a B-movie that was even worse than its title suggests. Then he wound up with top billing — though not, curiously, the lead role — in *Return of the Killer Tomatoes!*, the 1988 sequel to *Attack of the Killer Tomatoes*. Although *Return* was by no means a great film, it was one of those rare sequels that is better than the original despite the fact that it opened with gratuitous scenes of bikini-clad women bouncing along the beach to the tune of "Big Breasted Girls Go to the Beach and Take Their Tops Off." What's most unbelievable about the film is that Clooney was able to keep a straight face while reciting his idiotic lines, though there are moments in his performance as Matt Stevens, a lecherous pizza cook who must face the challenges of working in a pizzeria now that tomatoes have been outlawed, when he seems to be on the verge of cracking up.

He worked fairly steadily over the next few years, mostly on television, but didn't find much work as a big-screen actor. He did work alongside Michelle Pfeiffer's sister, Dedee, in *Red Surf*, but the success of that film can pretty much be measured by the number of people who even know that Michelle Pfeiffer has a sister. A couple of years later, in 1992, George did a cameo in a picture that his cousin Miguel was shooting called *The Harvest*. He took the part as a lark, never dreaming that, a few years later when he was finally a big name in Hollywood, the tabloid show *Hard Copy* would replay Clooney's unfortunate few moments in the film — he wore a platinum blonde wig and a tight dress while lip-synching Belinda Carlisle's "Heaven Is a Place on Earth" at a transvestite nightclub — and try to pass it off as a shocking revelation about his sordid past. He can laugh about it now, but only because Ferrer forces him to, reminding him in an *Us* interview that he didn't look all bad in his cross-dressing film debut, just "kinda sleazy. Like a chick you could party with until she got cute." He also came tantalizingly close to getting a very big break when he narrowly lost the part of a sexy young cowboy in *Thelma & Louise* to Brad Pitt.

Although he'd apparently missed his chance to get on the fast track that led Pitt from this small part to starring roles in *Legends of the Fall* and Robert Redford's *A River Runs Through It*, Clooney had by no means reached a dead end. He simply set his course along a different road, making a number of other

Clooney and Sela Ward in *Sisters*
FOTOS INTERNATIONAL / ARCHIVE PHOTOS

television appearances in the early '90s. He hoped that, despite his knowledge that there was "a huge chasm between television and film," as he told *Prime Time Live*, he'd somehow end up in the same lane as actors like Pitt before too long. He played a ridiculously coiffed construction worker in the ill-fated sitcom *Baby Talk*, and gained virtually no recognition for his work in the equally short-lived *Sunset Beat* (in which he played a character by the unfortunate name of Chic Chesbro).

But things eventually began to come together. A series of recurring roles — as Roseanne's loathsome boss on the first season of *Roseanne* and as a detective on *Bodies of Evidence* and *Sisters* — finally gained him some notice.

And the best was yet to come.

FOUR

WELCOME TO THE BIG TIME

By 1994, Clooney had spent a dozen long years in Hollywood and was gradually inching his way forward to something closely approximating an actual career as an actor. But as he took stock of where he'd been and where he was now, he couldn't help but feel that there was somewhere else he should still be going. As a matter of fact, his life now didn't feel all that much different from his early years on the West Coast. Sure, he'd gained a measure of financial security and independence, and had already made a number of good connections in the industry, but things somehow felt essentially the same as they had when he'd first rolled into town in the Danger Car. Twelve years ago he'd bounced from audition to audition hoping that one of them would lead to a part — any part — in an honest-to-goodness theatrical or studio production. Now, having reached the point at which he was landing such parts with some consistency, he was bouncing from soundstage to soundstage hoping that one of these roles — or even one of these shows — would last long enough for him to establish himself in the community.

Little did Clooney know that NBC had been developing an idea for a series pitched to them by Michael Crichton, whose clout in Hollywood had been confirmed by the box-office punch packed by the film adaptation of his best-selling novel *Jurassic Park*. Although NBC had made itself the network king of comedy over the past decade, it hadn't had a truly successful prime-time drama since *L.A. Law* left the air. The fact that its news-magazine program, *Dateline NBC*, was expanded to a second hour-long prime-time broadcast each week was a pretty good indication of how thoroughly unable the network was to plug a winning dramatic series into its fall lineup. Since in-house efforts to create such a show had stalled, the network obviously needed someone else to bring it a salable project. NBC Entertainment president Warren Littlefield's face must have lit up like a cash register on Christmas Eve when he received word that Crichton had made his pitch to the network with a show that would focus on the troubled lives of the doctors who battled in the trenches of an inner-city emergency room. And so, shortly after a series of tedious meetings between Crichton's people and NBC, the Chicago-born author was given the green light to begin developing a script for the as-yet-unnamed drama.

The reigning philosophy in contemporary Hollywood has been that the surest way to guarantee the success of a show is to build it around a marketable star. This trend explains the popularity of such programs as *Seinfeld*, *Frasier*, and the unfortunately titled *Everybody Loves Raymond*. Even the Fox network, which prefers to play the renegade in its approach to casting and programming, has jumped on board; its hit series *Millennium* was written with actor Lance Henriksen (*Alien*) in mind. But the development team

for the new collaboration between Crichton and NBC
didn't want to go this route for two reasons. First of
all, the show was clearly going to sink or swim as an
ensemble piece, and trying to build a strong ensemble
around a single actor almost never works. Second, the
show's creators wanted it to have a slightly rough-
hewn edge, and thought that the best way to achieve
this was to use relatively unknown actors.

George Clooney was, of course, as relatively unknown an actor as one was likely to find roaming the
streets of Hollywood. He was so unknown, in fact,
that he wasn't even called to audition for the show.
Instead, he heard about the project when a friend
who'd got his hands on an early draft of the script
handed it off to him. It was still a little sketchy, but as
Clooney pored over the script he started to get the
feeling that there was something special about it. He
guarded it jealously, acting almost like a little kid who
has discovered a treasure map and doesn't want anyone to get a look at it over his shoulder. Maybe it was
just that so many of the scripts he'd read up until
now were so bad that this one seemed so good. But
maybe not. What caught his eye in particular, he told
Biography, was the character of moody pediatrician
Doug Ross. "I like the flaws in this guy," Clooney
thought as he read and reread the script with increased
excitement. "I can play him."

He got on the phone to his agent and proclaimed
his intention to put everything else on hold and fight
like hell for this role. His agent had already heard
some of the industry buzz surrounding NBC's new pet
project, and was sure that the network wouldn't be
devoting this much energy to something unless it had
the legs to become television's next big thing, but he
was forced to preach caution to Clooney. Putting all

Hollywood — a risky proposition
S. MURPHY / SHOOTING STAR

of the actor's eggs in one Hollywood basket was a risky proposition, and it was much safer to keep a few in reserve just in case things didn't work out. He should have remembered whom he was talking to. Clooney was 12 years older and a little bit wiser, but he was still, deep down, the same guy who had thrown caution to the wind when he'd set out for Hollywood. The agent honored Clooney's wishes and got him an audition, which led to a callback and subsequent readings with some of the other actors NBC was looking at for the show.

Then came the magic phone call informing him that he'd got the part and needed to book an appointment to sign his five-year contract with Warner Bros. Television, which was co-producing the show. He would star as Dr. Doug Ross in NBC's new medical drama, ER.

Pressed to speculate aloud on what it was, exactly, that led to this climactic moment of good fortune, Clooney plays it coyly, attributing his success in a casually self-deprecating manner to little more than his hair, which started to grey rapidly when he hit 32. Suddenly he didn't look quite so boyish, and that change alone, he tells *Us* magazine, "is a huge benefit to me because, remember, I'm coming out of nowhere. Finally, after being the wrong age for everything, I am the *right* age for everything. I look like a man." His sudden change in appearance certainly didn't hurt his chances at all — he had always looked slightly uncomfortable in his awkwardly gangly body and glamor-boy haircut — but it couldn't account for everything. And although Clooney's natural small-town humility forced him to sell himself short, at least one person was quick to recognize the underlying reasons for his success. His father, no doubt beaming with pride at his son's accomplishment, knows that "[George's] talent dragged him by the nose to where he is now." Most importantly, however, the elder Clooney knows his son is truly deserving of the rewards Hollywood has to offer. "He's worked for it," he tells the *Columbus Dispatch* proudly.

Clooney spent his first few days on the Warner Bros. lot where ER is filmed getting to know his colleagues and easily ingratiating himself with those who worked in front of the camera and behind it. He, perhaps more than anyone else involved in the show, took immediate responsibility for creating a sense of family on the set, and achieved his goal by acting like the pesky kid brother that the entire cast had never known it had. His antics kept everyone loose and in good humor, which were vital to the mental health of a group of actors who not only had to master handling unfamiliar instruments and a new vocabulary which included such unfathomable (and nearly unpronounceable) terms as sensory ganglionitis, cholesteatoma, and myasthenia gravis, but also had to do so while spending 15-hour days on the set beginning each morning at 6:00. Even executive producer John Wells acknowledges to *Entertainment Weekly Online* that one of the biggest problems the cast and crew of the show encounter is "not having enough rest."

If there was one valuable lesson Clooney had learned during his 12-year Hollywood apprenticeship, he tells *Prime Time Live*, it was that "if you are a pain in the ass then it's going to be an un-fun set to be on, period." His constant joking around was a preemptive strike designed to deflect any potential pains in the ass. Without it, those days surely would have seemed even longer than they already were, and the actors quite likely would have been at one another's throats by the third day of rehearsal.

Clooney relieves his own job-related stress in much the same way that his character does on the show. After a long day of treating sick kids and banging his head against the brick wall of the hospital's bureaucracy, Doug Ross most often takes out his frustrations on the basketball court located just outside the ambulance entrance to County General's emergency room. It's here that his character landed all those hard fouls on the hapless John Carter after sleeping with his girlfriend, Harper Tracy. It's also the place where he and Mark Greene have had, in the casual way that only guys can have them, some of their most important, soul-searching conversations. But in real life, the basketball court is just the place where George Clooney escapes the daily grind of rehearsing and taping the show and kicks some major butt.

It's not surprising that Clooney would be a hoops hound. While it's true that his childhood dream was to suit up and head out onto the baseball diamond with the Cincinnati Reds, no young boy raised in the Bluegrass State could help but be interested in basketball. Kentucky was basketball's heartland, the place where the University of Kentucky Wildcats, under legendary head coach Adolf Rupp (and more recently under Rick Pitino before he lit out to coach the Boston Celtics), had built a venerable tradition of basketball excellence. Only Clooney's comparatively small stature kept him from pursuing the sport at the organized level. College hoops star Joel Baetz, known as a ferocious rebounder himself, says that Clooney's greatest attribute as a basketball player is his pure aggression and nose for the ball. He'll fight through double-teams composed of much taller athletes just to get his hand on any ball that careens off the backboard. And unlike Dennis Rodman, the NBA star who is known almost as well for his multicolored hairdos as for his incredible rebounding, Clooney can shoot too. He's smart and quick enough to get possession of the ball, fake an outlet pass, and then get outside the key to launch one of his patented outside shots.

Not many of the people he plays against on the set can match his on-court talents. One of his regular competitors on the Warner Bros. lot is Jaleel White, better known as the annoying Steve Urkel on *Family Matters*. White, who is quite tall and much more athletic than the character he portrays on his sitcom, can hold his own in the games of one-on-one he plays with Clooney, but he tells *Entertainment Weekly* that most other actors who wish to join in "don't stand a chance" when faced with Clooney's multifaceted game. Clooney even proved himself capable of whipping the

Clooney limps into the Golden Globe
awards, with Celine Balitran on his arm

REED SAXON / AP/WIDE WORLD PHOTOS

Man of Steel's butt at his favorite game. While filming
Batman and Robin on the Warner Bros. lot, he had
occasion to shoot hoops with Dean Cain, then the star
of ABC's *Lois and Clark: The New Adventures of Superman*. In fact, when asked what he thought was the
best thing about being Batman, he bragged to *Cinescape*, "I get to kick the *hell* out of Superman."

Clooney also wields a pretty mean tennis racket, and he's a decent golfer who plays with a 13 handicap. But he reserves these sports for those rare times when he can avail himself of a little relaxation. It's basketball that keeps him juiced up and, maybe even more importantly, keeps his weight down. Because of the multiple injuries Clooney has suffered due to his gung-ho style of hoops play — injuries that include a sprained ankle that kept him in crutches, a gash over his eyebrow, and a ruptured eye socket — his bosses feared he would soon resemble the bandaged, blood-smeared extras who stroll nonchalantly across the set when they're not in character and being worked on by a member of Cook County's medical staff. Sure, Clooney was getting to be a fine actor, but his matinee-idol good looks certainly didn't scare many viewers away, and the studio didn't much care to see its investment jeopardized by a flailing elbow or ill-timed pass. Clooney rebuffed suggestions that he find a less hazardous pastime by laying it on the line for an *Us* interviewer: "Hey, do you want a fat Batman? Because I put on weight easily. You have to get into a regimen. And in my regimen, I play ball."

Clooney's other favorite sport is testing his friends' patience with practical jokes. His gags range in size and complexity from such minor-league tricks as putting surgical lubricant on a telephone and handing the receiver to an unwitting victim or walking up behind a person and pretending to sneeze while spraying bottled water on the back of his or her neck to pranks of such proportions that they must be carefully set in motion over days or even weeks. There was the time, for instance, that he had his personal assistant, Amy Cohen, fly to Las Vegas and spy on a friend who had somehow done Clooney wrong. She came back with a lovely snapshot of the friend, obviously drunk and cavorting with a very sexy young woman. Clooney then forwarded a copy of the photo to the guy's girlfriend, letting the chips fall where they may. Noah Wyle clearly knows what he's talking about when he calls Clooney, on *Prime Time Live*, "one of the most vicious practical jokers I've ever met."

Although this prank had a malevolent side to it, most of George's capers are all in good fun, just good-natured guy stuff that he usually only pulls on people whom he knows can laugh at themselves. There was the time, for example, when he asked a member of the show's support staff whether it might be possible to include some hardboiled eggs on the lunch table each day. She complied, and cast and crew would nonchalantly nosh on eggs during a break in the action. Clooney let them get comfortable with this addition to the menu for a few days before coming in early one morning and replacing the hardboiled eggs with raw ones. All that was left after that was to sit back and howl at the results as the first few suckers cracked open their eggs and ended up with goo all over their hands.

Clooney is so proficient with eggs, in fact, that the Egg Information Board should consider signing him on as a sponsor. Although he's no whiz in the kitchen, one of his favorite uses for them is as projectiles. His arm may not have been good enough to secure him a spot on the Cincinnati Reds, but it's plenty powerful and accurate enough to get the job done when he has a hankering to give someone's house or car his own special egg bath. "They're the perfect bomb," he confides to the *Us* interviewer with an evil grin. "They're aerodynamic. They feel so good in your hand. They look beautiful going through the air. They make a great sound when they hit. And if you don't clean them up, they really, really stink." Not exactly words likely to garner him a nomination for most mature actor in a dramatic series, but this natural boyishness is fundamental to the charm that Clooney demonstrates in everyday life and injects into Doug Ross's character on the show.

Much like a teenage boy, Clooney revels in telling anybody who'll take the time to listen about his latest escapades. Sometimes it's hard to tell which he likes better: the look on his victim's face after he's successfully pulled off another practical joke or the look on his listener's face as he does an admirably detailed play-by-play of the prank in question. Anthony Edwards, who has served as victim and listener on a number of occasions, marvels at the gusto with which Clooney narrates his life of whoopee-cushioning crime. "I just picture George's brain as this incredible filing system of funny anecdotes about the things he's done," he explains in an *Us* interview. "But even if you've heard the story 500 times, he tells it so well that you can't help but laugh." And this cast and crew, which had been pouring their blood, sweat, and tears into ER during the months of rehearsal and taping that preceded its first season, needed all the laughs they could get.

When the show finally hit the air with a two-hour pilot titled "24 Hours," it created an almost immediate splash in the ratings and with the critics. It soon proved that it didn't much need its cushy Thursday-evening time slot, doing away with competing shows such as CBS's *Chicago Hope* and ABC's *Prime Time Live* in short order by attracting 25 million viewers per week. By mid-season, it had proven itself as a reliable top-10 show in the weekly Neilsen ratings, and it finished its first season as the third-highest-ranked show — and top-rated drama — in the country. Not surprisingly, ER was rewarded with some hardware at the end of the season, winning the Emmy for Outstanding Drama Series. Unfortunately, Clooney was unsuccessful in his bid for the Emmy for Best Actor in a Drama Series, for which he and co-star Anthony Edwards were both nominated.

But how upset could he be about not being singled out for his performances in a series that had such a remarkably fine ensemble cast? Grousing about not receiving awards for his portrayal of Doug Ross would have been the equivalent of complaining that his parents hadn't proclaimed him their favorite child. It just wouldn't be right, especially given the fact that he was so bad at remembering lines that he sometimes affixed them to gurneys so he could cheat if necessary. Besides, if one person had to be singled out for his contribution to the show, that person would have to be Edwards, who, as Dr. Mark Greene, was as close to being the show's center of attention as was possible in this kind of project. It was unfortunate, then, that a tabloid concocted a story about Edwards and Clooney not getting along on the set, spinning the yarn out to such great effect that it was soon picked up by shows like *Hard Copy* and *Inside Edition*, which wove scandalous stories of their own from the material, pegging Clooney as the good-looking prima donna who wanted to put the nerdy Edwards in his place. It was just this kind of bad press that the network's powers-that-be had hoped to avoid by designing strict guidelines governing publicity shots, which had to feature certain combinations of the ensemble.

But even if the two actors hadn't been such good friends by the time the "story" broke, no one on the set would have bought it for a second. Least of all

Clooney and pal Anthony Edwards
RON DAVIS / SHOOTING STAR

Edwards, who dispels any notion that Clooney's attitude could use some corrective surgery. "George has set a really wonderful example of *not* becoming a jerk movie star," he tells *Vanity Fair*. "He's not ego-tripping. He is solid with himself that he hasn't changed." In fact, Edwards goes on to say on *Prime Time Live*, Clooney is "an incredibly kind of soppy, faithful friend to a great group of people, and George is consistently gracious and caring for other people in ways that are not typical for big stars."

Clooney is the guy, after all, who gave the keys to his treasured 1960 Oldsmobile Dynamic 88 to co-star Noah Wyle (Dr. John Carter) as a gift, telling the young actor that he hoped some of the good luck the car had brought him would rub off on its new owner. He is the guy about whom Julianna Margulies (Nurse Carol Hathaway) says in *Entertainment Weekly*, "If I was stuck somewhere in Alaska at four in the morning without any money and I was in jail, I would call George." He is a guy who sums up his own contribution to the show for *Entertainment Weekly Online* in typical self-deprecating fashion by asking, "You know how girls work together and then all of a sudden they have periods all at the same time? It's kind of that way. You kind of blend into the same sort of style. I steal from everybody." So much for all that family discord.

One of the show's greatest successes in its opening season was its ability to communicate that sense of family to its viewers. Executive Producer Wells speaks for cast, crew, and home audience alike when he offers *Entertainment Weekly Online* this appraisal of ER's actors: "They make it someplace you want to show up every week. You want to spend time with these people." Michael Crichton had been adamant from the moment he first pitched the idea to NBC that the show's focus be on the lives of the doctors, and not on the diseases they were treating each week. Wells agreed that viewers were more likely to be hooked by well-constructed characters than by complicated illnesses and grisly injuries, though the show would certainly offer plenty of these to satisfy the appetites of its viewers. The real challenge, as Crichton and Wells saw it, was to make the lives of the characters as engrossing as the feats of medical magic they would perform in each episode.

Clooney horses around with Noah Wyle

RON DAVIS / SHOOTING STAR

It's to the credit of both the writers and the actors that ER has, from the beginning, lived up on two levels to NBC Entertainment president Warren Littlefield's *Online* description of it as "a roller coaster ride that goes from 100 miles per hour almost to a dead stop, and then starts back up again." First, the show packs so much out-and-out action into each episode that it could give an adrenalin rush to a corpse. Gurneys bearing maimed and mutilated patients roll across the screen at an almost mind-boggling rate, and each case becomes a miniature drama itself. Second, the private and professional lives of the doctors themselves are strapped in for the very same ride, taking wild turns and making abrupt stops that leave even the cast breathless. Noah Wyle describes for *Online* what it feels like to be part of television's medical thrill ride: "When we get scripts, we pore over them, trying to find good stuff [to figure out] who the hell we're playing. And there have been times that we're like, 'Oh, Lewis has a sister!' 'Oh, look at that, Dr. Greene's got a mom!' We were in episode 12 before George knew he had a son, episode 14 before I knew I had a brother — and they killed him by 17." If the cast could get this excited about what was going to happen next week, is it any wonder that nearly 10 percent of the population of the United States was eager to come along with them for the ride?

But there is a risk in ushering hordes of people into the roller coaster each week, and that risk is that, after a while, the ride won't seem nearly as thrilling as it did at first. That's why, heading into their second season, the entire cast and crew were served notice that their official mantra was, as Wyle repeats in the same interview, "Our biggest competition is our first season, not any other show." While members of the cast were

given the usual summer hiatus to recoup their energy,
the writing staff took only a two-week break before
launching into work for the second season's story
lines. The result of their efforts was a second season
that easily lived up to the promise of the first. What's
more, Clooney was figuring more prominently in
the show's main narrative as Doug Ross battled his
demons and emerged as the most compelling anti-
hero that television had produced in quite some time.
The climactic moment for his character came in "Hell
and High Water," the episode in which Ross struggles
to save a drowning boy and, metaphorically, himself.
More importantly, this episode showed that Clooney
wasn't merely along for the ride — he was at its
controls.

The only question now was how long he'd be willing to stay there. His name was on the lips of all the
Hollywood bigwigs, who were clambering over one
another to attach that name to one or more of their
projects. There were fears that he might bow out of
his contract to pursue a big-time movie career, as David
Caruso had done when he severed his ties, acrimoni-
ously, with ABC's NYPD Blue. Clooney, however, nipped
these rumors in the bud, telling a Biography journalist
that as far as he was concerned, honoring his contract
with the network was simply "the right thing to do."
Even if ER's executive producer hadn't been willing
to make scheduling accommodations should Clooney
wish to sneak away and do some other work, he would
have stayed put. Sure, he wanted to end up with a big
studio deal someday — what actor didn't? But he'd
spent too long working to get to this point in his career
to risk it, as Caruso had, by walking away: "I don't
think of ER as a stepping stone, but as a landing zone.
This is what you fight to get into, not what you fight

to get out of." And Clooney had won the most important fight of all: remaining true to himself and his values as he honored his commitment to appear in the show's third season.

But with the offers to appear in major motion pictures mounting, the question now was how much longer he would be able to fight his own destiny.

FIVE

BY GEORGE, I THINK HE'S A MOVIE STAR!

It didn't take very long for the rest of Hollywood to figure out that Clooney was the real deal. He suddenly found himself in the enviable position of being able to turn down offers from studios that at one time wouldn't have given him so much as the time of day. He wasn't just holding out in order to exact some kind of petty vengeance for having been overlooked in the past — his mother had drilled into him as a child the dangers of, as she would say, "cutting off your nose to spite your face." If anything, turning down the offers that began pouring in after the first season of ER frightened him just a little. Did he really know what he was doing when he rejected an offer to appear in a film for a cool $1 million? He declines now to say who, exactly, offered him the chance to become an instant millionaire, admitting to *Entertainment Weekly Online* only that he turned down the part because he didn't want to be the guy who took a chance at a "big payday, got a lot of attention, and then went into a bad film."

Nick and Nina's only son was no dummy. You didn't have to be a Vegas card shark to know that you can only gamble successfully for so long before it's time to grab your winnings and deposit them in a nice, safe place. He was worried that the next risk he took might be his last, and thought it best just to stay put for a while and see how things developed. His sudden celebrity, and the constant requests that he sit for an interview, make himself available for a photo opportunity, or take the time to read just these few scripts made him feel, oddly enough, like one of America's Most Wanted. It was as if he had, by stealing hearts and Neilsen ratings on ER, just pulled off the crime of the century. The best thing to do was lie low for a little while and let some of the heat die down before sticking his neck out again. The last thing he could afford to do right now was become greedy.

Or maybe that was just the second-to-last thing he could afford to do. The *very last* thing he could afford to do was believe his own hype. Not that this would be easy. His life, which had always seemed a rather humdrum affair to him until he got belted into the ER joyride, now consisted of a series of reminders that he was one famous dude. He and Anthony Edwards would discuss the culture shock that came along with being granted sudden membership in what they called "the famous club," whose privileges include not only the best seats in Hollywood's poshest restaurants, but also the attention of enough autograph seekers and photo hounds to make the likelihood of enjoying such perks quite remote. Still, despite the army of admirers that now seemed to follow Clooney wherever he went, it was a simple "hello" from another actor, and not the deafening screams of the mob, that made him realize that he had made it big. Clooney recounts the

Clooney with other "famous club" members
— Sandra Bullock and Bill Pullman

GREGG DEGUIRE / LONDON FEATURES

story on *Prime Time Live*: "I remember I met James
Woods, such a great actor, and I'm walking down and
I go, 'Hi, James Woods,' and he goes, 'Hi, George.'
And I go, 'Hmph — he knew who I was. I'm in the
famous club.'"

But Clooney was aware that few stars were offered
lifetime membership in the club, and he knew better
than to be smug and self-satisfied about his current
status. In addition to having seen his father proclaimed
the toast of one Cincinnati town after the other only
to be shipped out, inevitably, to some other station
where he'd have to start all over again, he's learned
from the example of his aunt. Rosemary had certainly
spent a lot more than 15 minutes in the famous club,
but she was quickly shown the door when, for whatever reason, her singing style no longer captivated the
public as it once had. "My aunt was very famous and

then very unfamous," Clooney tells a *Biography* interviewer, contemplating his own star status. "Not that she became a worse singer along the way. Things just change."

A person's reputation in show business is only as good as the popularity of his or her last project, no matter how high the quality of the work. The collective memory of Hollywood's high-powered residents is so short that the town motto might as well be "What have you done for me lately?" In order to avoid falling behind in the rat race that had claimed his aunt, Clooney decided that he wasn't just going to leap out of the gates at the crack of the starter's pistol. He'd take his time, reminding himself at every turn as he circled the Hollywood track at his own pace that, as he puts it for *Tribute*, "You're never as good as they say you are, and you're never as bad as they say you are." His challenge, as he saw it, was to put the blinders on and just keep pushing forward, ignoring the Hollywood hype machine and taking care of business in his own way.

But he could only shut out the rising clamor that surrounded him for so long before he would have to give in. As bad as rushing into something might be, he couldn't stand on the sidelines forever, waiting for someone to call him into the game with the promise of a can't-miss play designed exclusively for him. Sooner or later he'd have to step onto the court, post up against the defense, and try to take his best shot. Because as absolutely unassailable as ER's place in the ratings seemed right now, all good series must come to an end, and Clooney had no intention of being left high and dry when the show, as would be inevitable, sailed off into the distance for a life of reruns. He and his agent sorted through the pile of scripts he'd been offered and decided that a weird-sounding vampire flick that director Robert Rodriguez was working on might be an interesting possibility.

The story that the script for *From Dusk till Dawn* told was downright crazy, tracing the bloody trail of two psychopathic brothers who commandeer an RV and take its owner and his family hostage and cross the border into Mexico and end up at an eerie truck stop at dusk and go in and rough up the customers and find themselves fighting vampires and then turning into vampires themselves and then . . . Whew! It's dawn again, and things return to normal. The casual observer may find it hard to understand why Clooney would even consider turning in his stethoscope to take part in such an apparent fiasco, but to him it made perfect sense. First there was the script, which, weird as it was, had been written by Quentin Tarantino, the much-ballyhooed director of *Reservoir Dogs* and *Pulp Fiction*. Clooney had worked with him previously when Tarantino had taken the helm for an episode of ER ("Motherhood," aired in the show's first season), and the actor had liked working under Tarantino's manic directorial system — and liked his sense of humor even more. And although Tarantino would be acting in this movie instead of directing it — that chore would be handled by Rodriguez, the director of the stylishly violent cult hits *El Mariachi* and *Desperado* — Clooney was looking forward to working with him again.

The second consideration was the rest of the cast, which included acclaimed actors such as grizzled veteran Harvey Keitel (*Taxi Driver*, *The Piano*, and *Smoke*) and young workhorse Juliette Lewis (*Cape Fear*, *Husbands and Wives*, and *Natural Born Killers*). Working with these big-name stars was part of the attraction,

Clooney and Quentin Tarantino
J. RUDOLPH, DIMENSION / SHOOTING STAR

but even more valuable to Clooney was the opportunity to fit into an ensemble cast instead of being expected to carry a picture on his own. He'd seen this strategy in action before while on the set of *Roseanne.* Lori Metcalf, who played Roseanne's sister Jackie on the sitcom, would take small parts in big pictures such as *Internal Affairs* and Oliver Stone's *JFK*, and Clooney would think, as he tells *Entertainment Weekly Online,* "That's the perfect way to go, because eventually the TV series goes away." If he could follow Metcalf's example and get away to do some big-screen work without jeopardizing his place on ER, he could, maybe, enjoy the best of both worlds.

After spending a couple of long months doing double duty, splitting his time (with Executive Producer John Wells's blessing) between the sets of ER and *From Dusk till Dawn,* Clooney finally had a little downtime while he was waiting for the film to be released. Or at least he *thought* he'd have some downtime. Unbeknownst to him, Rodriguez, who was supposed to be busy editing the footage for the film, had taken time to put together some clips featuring plenty of shots of Clooney and a bunch of fake reviews for the movie. He then sent them around town to stir up interest in the film and its good-looking star. When the buzz had circulated long enough to find its way to Clooney himself, he called Rodriguez to see what was up. The director placated Clooney by giving him a lesson in how things really get done in Hollywood. "All we need to do is send bootleg footage around town and people will want to see it and we'll get everybody stirred up about you," Clooney quotes Rodriguez as saying for *Online.* Rodriguez reminded him that publicity — even manufactured publicity — was the name of the game in Hollywood. "You'll be a millionaire before the movie even comes out. I did the same thing with Antonio Banderas right after we wrapped *Desperado,* and that's how he got *Assassins.*"

Rodriguez's strategy was brash, and even a little insulting to the actors whose careers he'd claimed to invigorate, but Clooney couldn't do much more than play along with the scheme — no matter how profoundly uncomfortable it made him feel. Here he'd been, preaching the dangers of believing his own hype all this time, and now he felt complicit in creating it. But as unsure as he might have been about the style and motives of this publicity campaign, he could hardly argue with its results. Before *From Dusk till Dawn* even hit the nation's theaters, he had agreed to an offer worth a reported $3 million to shoot a romantic comedy, *One Fine Day,* with Michelle Pfeiffer. He had also been offered, and very nearly accepted, an equivalent sum to play the title role in *The Green Hornet* with Jason Scott Lee. He would have taken the latter role were it not for the fact that Steven Spielberg, who just happens to be the head honcho at Amblin Entertainment, which co-produces ER, had his eye on Clooney for the first picture to be produced under the banner of Spielberg's new super studio, DreamWorks SKG. And when the big man comes a-calling, Clooney knew, saying no just wasn't an option.

Looking back on things now, Clooney is probably grateful for Rodriguez's subterfuge. *From Dusk till Dawn* didn't exactly set any box-office records, so it wasn't the dependable career vehicle that Rodriguez had claimed it would be. In fact, the movie was almost universally panned by the critics, who thought it a cartoonish waste of time, money, and talent. Fortunately, nobody was holding Clooney responsible for the movie's failings. Indeed, his performance as psycho Seth Gecko was being hailed as its one redeeming feature, although the clear message being sent by most critics was that Clooney should avoid such roles in the future if he hoped to become a real movie star. But he'd already figured this out for himself. He didn't regret shooting the splatter flick at all, because it had given him the chance to play a character who was light years removed from Doug Ross. But he also hoped that he wouldn't feel compelled to get involved in a similar project anytime soon.

If playing Seth Gecko had forced Clooney to take a 180-degree turn away from the types of characters he'd played in the past, then his next role allowed him to turn again toward more familiar territory. In *One Fine Day*, he played Jack Taylor, a divorced columnist for the New York *Daily News*, opposite Michelle Pfeiffer, the sultry star of *The Witches of Eastwick, The Fabulous Baker Boys*, and, more recently, *Dangerous*

Minds. The movie didn't provide Clooney with much opportunity to expand his range as an actor — it was, after all, just another nice, safe romantic comedy — but it did give him some great exposure in a lovable role. The movie did well enough at the box office, and won him a friend in Pfeiffer, who had a big say in Clooney landing the role in the first place. She attests to the fact that he was so well suited for the part that memorizing his lines was probably the biggest challenge that it offered him. "We sat down and had a meeting," she remembers, "and it became clear to me in about ten or fifteen minutes that he was really this character and that he really had everything that he needed: he was charming and he was funny." She goes on to tell *Mr. Showbiz Interview* that he "could be a little bit of a dick-head and be charming at the same time. And all of that was important." In other words, all he had to do was be himself. Not a bad way to earn $3 million, even if it did mean being a little bit of a dick-head.

After the filming of *One Fine Day* was complete, Clooney was off to eastern Europe to shoot Dream-Works SKG's first picture, *The Peacemaker*, with Nicole Kidman. Trading in his dictionary of medical terms for a primer on military lingo, Clooney played the leader of an elite U.S. military unit charged with the responsibility of keeping track of nuclear arms all over the world and making sure they didn't fall into the wrong hands. The movie landed at the top of the box-office heap on its first weekend in release in September of 1997, and immediately became the center of a storm of controversy. It isn't often that an action-suspense movie inspires serious thought and conversation, but this one did. Newspapers, magazines, and serious television call-in shows such as

CNN's *Talkback Live* were suddenly assembling panels of esteemed experts to discuss the possibility of nuclear arms being traded on the global market for the purpose of waging a war of terror on the United States.

Clooney's performance in the film nearly got lost in the media shuffle, which would have marked the second time in two movies that this had happened. The first, of course, involved *Batman and Robin*, a movie that, despite the hundreds of millions of dollars it will eventually make in worldwide release, was deemed a failure because it lacked the box-office punch of its predecessors. Within two months of its release, Warner Bros. announced it would not back another Batman flick, thus virtually guaranteeing that Clooney would not be given the opportunity to reprise his role as the caped crusader. Some camps were quick to point the finger at Clooney, saying that he didn't have what it took to carry a picture on his back. David Letterman summed up the cynical attitude held by those who blamed Clooney for the movie's lackluster showing when he quipped sarcastically to his *Late Show* audience, after telling them of the Warner Bros. decision, "Thanks a lot, Clooney."

This had, of course, been Clooney's fear long before *Batman and Robin* had its premiere: that he would have to take the rap if the film didn't live up to the success of its predecessors. Going into the project, he'd thought that his job, plain and simple, was "not to screw up something that's worked three other times," as he told *Tribute*. He entered into the deal with Warner Bros. in good faith, and worked hard to ensure that the latest edition of Batman would be a memorable one. Although he had joked, when asked what he would bring to the character, that he would play "the over-stupid Batman," the truth is that he fought hard in script meetings for the right to play a Batman — or at least a Bruce Wayne — who wasn't as consumed by depression as he'd been in the earlier films. He didn't necessarily envision a return to the more or less idiotic caped crusader of the television series, but he did think it was time for Batman to lighten up. "We tried to get rid of some of the moodiness that Batman had in the other movies," Clooney explains in *Cinescape*. "I mean, let's think about it for a minute. Batman does not have such a tough life. The guy is loaded. He gets all the best girls. He has a cool car. What does Batman have to be depressed about?" What, indeed? Unless, of course, he held some Warner Bros. stock and saw its value depreciate after the new Batman swooped onto screens across North America.

Clooney with Joel Schumacher and cast of *Batman and Robin*
PETER JORDAN / AP/WIDE WORLD PHOTOS

But all the attempts to pin blame on Clooney inevitably failed. First of all, as director Joel Schumacher said himself, Clooney did as good a job in the role as Michael Keaton or Val Kilmer had. Schumacher even went so far as to tell *Prime Time Live*, "I think George Clooney is the best Batman, for me, and the best Bruce Wayne, because he has brought a humanity to the piece that wasn't there before." But what Schumacher had seemed to lose sight of — perhaps because he was so eager to get in yet another dig at Kilmer — was that the success of the Batman movies had less to do with the man behind the mask than the vision behind the entire project. And unfortunately, Schumacher's vision in *Batman and Robin* seemed to have more to do with overwhelming the audience with startlingly beautiful sets and special effects than bothering with such things as believable action and intelligible dialogue.

Clooney's saving grace was that he had known all along, as he says to a *Biography* interviewer, that "Batman isn't the most interesting character in the Batman projects," even if Schumacher didn't. And despite playing along with Schumacher's routine about *Batman and Robin* being Clooney's big shot at a big-time movie career, he was sure, deep down, that he couldn't be held entirely accountable for the fortunes of a film whose main character was put through its most memorable paces by a stunt double, and not by Clooney at all. He did feel a measure of responsibility for the movie's poor showing — maybe he could have fought harder for script changes — but he wasn't about to beat himself up about it. God knows he had an entire industry willing to do that for him.

But even though he could hear the terrifying sound of the critics sharpening their knives to take a piece out of him, Clooney was never subjected to the

vicious slicing apart of his career prospects that other
actors in similar positions — David Caruso's name
leaps immediately to mind — had suffered. The critics
sheathed their blades where Clooney was concerned
because they recognized two things. First, of all the
failings the film could be accused of, Clooney's performance wasn't one of them. Second, and perhaps
even more important, even the critics recognized
Clooney as a good guy, and they didn't want to be
implicated in manufacturing his demise out of such
flimsy material as *Batman and Robin* had to offer.

But there would be others who were eager enough
to do just that.

FIGHTING THE GOOD FIGHT

One of Clooney's most admirable qualities has always been his willingness to take the feelings of others into account before doing or saying anything that might hurt or upset them. Some of the victims of his evil practical jokes might disagree with this evaluation of his character, but those close to him will affirm that he exercises restraint whenever necessary. No one has been the brunt of his humor more than Julianna Margulies, and, as corny as it may sound, even she admits, in *Movieline*'s Internet site, "I feel like I have a big brother watching out for me" in George. He also watched out for Alicia Silverstone during the filming of *Batman and Robin*, taking care not to needle her too much because he knew she was going through a tough time with a media that had suddenly turned on her, calling her fat for no reason other than to sell some papers. Clooney didn't quite treat her with kid gloves — he had to hit her with the occasional zinger to let her know that he thought she was all right — but made sure to consider her feelings before having too much fun at her expense.

This was only the most recent sign of Clooney's compassion, which Schumacher had noticed soon after meeting him. "I think anyone who has been locked out for a while, who has been rejected, suffers," Schumacher tells *Us*. "And I think that kind of suffering doesn't *build* character, it *reveals* it. Once some people get successful, they emerge as bitter and resentful. In George's case, I think, he's grateful for the opportunities he has now." More to the point, he could appreciate how hard other people had to work to get ahead in this crazy business, and he really didn't see the need for the media to kick someone when he or she was down. Clooney's hard-fought fame and fortune only made him wish all the more that his friends in the business could share in his success. "I wish those things would happen for them. It would be fun," he explains to an *In Style* journalist, taking care to add, just so things don't get too heavy, that "then they wouldn't want to borrow money from me."

What he didn't wish for his friends — what he wouldn't have wished upon his worst enemy — was the attention of the tabloid media that would hound them should they attain his level of renown. It seemed that anyone who dared to be successful in this town was doomed to be tested, and sometimes even destroyed, by the "journalists" who would spend their time rooting around in closets for skeletons or, should they be unable to find any, simply fabricating stories designed for maximum embarrassment with minimum credibility. He had seen the effects the tabloids could have on the lives of big stars when he worked on *Roseanne* during its first season and witnessed the barrage of cruel stories that would be run about its star and co-creator in such rags as the *National Enquirer* and their television counterparts *Hard Copy*, *American Journal*, and *A Current Affair*. Being so compassionate himself, he found it hard to comprehend how anyone could be so willfully cruel just to make a quick buck. But, having grown up with a father who practically exuded journalistic integrity, he liked to believe that he would be spared the slings and arrows of outrageous reporting.

He wasn't overly concerned about the early hits he took in the media, stories about him feuding with Anthony Edwards or ridiculous attempts to pass off footage from his appearances as a transvestite in *The Harvest* as part of his secret sexual past. Even stories about his life as a party animal didn't bother him too much. They were true, after all. So why not just play along, admitting, as he does now in GQ, "I've slept with too many women, I've done too many drugs, and I've been to too many parties." The best defense, he thought, was a good offense, so he figured that his wisest strategy was to be as candid about his bad-boy days as possible, thereby giving the tabloids nothing left to report.

He thought he himself could control how his name was circulated in the press, but his own good nature caused him to underestimate the willingness of other people to try to ruin him for no reason other than their own entertainment — and perhaps, of course, the couple of thousand bucks a tabloid journal or television show might offer for a damaging tidbit of information on him. He ignored the weekly stories that were told about him being seen with this woman and then that woman at this restaurant and then that awards show. He even turned a blind eye to a story that claimed he was a great womanizer, up to a point, but that his performances in bed were usually cut short because of his perpetual drunkenness. That sort of thing hurt Clooney to some degree, but it came with the territory, he thought, and didn't do any more harm to anyone's career or reputation than simple gossip would have done back in Kentucky. He could let it slide.

Things started to heat up, however, after the *L.A. Times* printed a story about him uttering a racial slur on the set of ER. The newspaper had got hold of the story after a woman from the set of the show filed a complaint with the Anti-Defamation League of the B'nai B'rith and, in its zeal to scoop other media outlets with the story, ran the item without bothering to corroborate her story with witnesses. Suddenly Clooney was being called an out-and-out racist by a reputable newspaper, and he'd never been given the opportunity to defend himself at all.

What he did next was a stroke of genius. Making use of his actor's smarts and his joker's cleverness, he called the B'nai B'rith and, without identifying himself by name, told them he was an Irish American who had been slandered when a private association leaked a defamatory story about him to the press. When the organization's representative asked him who had leaked the uncorroborated story, Clooney told him, as he recounts for *George* magazine, "It's the Anti-Defamation League of the B'nai B'rith. My name is George Clooney, and I want to know what you're going to do about it." When no one else would back up the story, the B'nai B'rith issued a full apology, and a retraction was eventually printed in the *Times*.

Things returned to normal for a while before Clooney embarked on his one-man crusade against the tabloids in 1996. He'd recently begun his first serious relationship in a number of years with a pretty young French woman named Celine Balitran, and he was finding the media crush surrounding him and his newfound love a little hard to take. It wasn't so much for his sake that he was angry as for hers. She wasn't acquainted with the media circus that insisted on setting up its tents without respect for a celebrity's privacy, and she was distressed by the shouts and sudden camera flashes that seemed to follow her and Clooney wherever they went. One media source even manufactured a story about her causing problems on the set of *Batman and Robin* by casting threatening glances at Elle Macpherson, who played Clooney's girlfriend in the film, at every opportunity. It didn't matter that none of this was true — despite the comments attributed to Macpherson, who, a *Globe and Mail* source claimed, "was shaking with nerves" whenever Balitran entered the room. Balitran was enjoying a relationship with one of Hollywood's best-loved leading men, and now she'd have to pay the price for falling in love, whether she liked it or not, as the tabloids manufactured their weekly stories about how vindictive and manipulative she was.

What these purveyors of lies didn't take into account, however, was how fiercely Clooney would stand by his woman. He tired quickly of Balitran's treatment in the media and the rude — and even dangerous — actions of aggressive videographers who wouldn't give them a moment's peace, and he'd be damned if he wasn't going to do something about it. But what could he do? He had plenty of clout with his fans and in the entertainment industry by now, but what good would it do him in this case? How could all the entertainment power in the world help him to take on the news media?

Then it hit him. He'd been wrong in thinking the entertainment and journalism industries were separate entities at all. Now that he thought of it, he realized that one of the shows that seemed to take special pride in trying to ruin his life, *Hard Copy*, was in fact owned by Paramount Domestic Television, which also owned the fluffy Hollywood promotional vehicle *Entertainment Tonight*. He'd done plenty of interviews with *ET* to promote *ER* and his movies, but had very little to show for his goodwill. So, in January 1996, he sent a letter to the show's producers telling them how he felt about helping Paramount make money on *ET*, which only got rolled over to produce *Hard Copy*, whose producers would shell out money to amateur videographers who would do almost anything to secure valuable footage of Clooney and other stars. It was this side of the business that really bugged Clooney. "I'm perfectly willing to take my hits if I'm caught doing something stupid," he asserts in an interview with *Time*. "The problem is that some of these guys aren't professional videographers; they're a bunch of kids with videocams who try and force you into a confrontation. They'll push you and yell volatile things like, 'Hey, George, who's the fat chick?' Or I'm walking with a guy, and they ask, 'Is that your gay lover?' And as soon as you say, 'Why, you son of a bitch!' they sell it to *Hard Copy*." He had, for some reason, put up with it until now, but he refused to help finance his own bad press a minute longer.

Then he got a frantic phone call from Frank Kelly, a senior president at Paramount. Kelly tried desperately to placate Clooney, offering to ensure that Clooney would never again find himself part of a *Hard Copy* story as long as he agreed to continue making appearances on *Entertainment Tonight*. Clooney, trying hard to imagine his father — or any other semi-reputable journalist — making such a concession, found Kelly's offer fantastic, but he said that he'd agree to the bargain as long as he got it in writing.

The letter came a few days later, and, true to his word, Kelly promised in it that *"Hard Copy* will not be covering [Clooney] in any future stories." He also wrote that he could "see no reason why there should be any areas of conflict in the future." Clooney framed the letter, which he described for *Mr. Showbiz Interview* as "a pretty amazing document," and hung it on a wall where he could see it clearly while faithfully watching *Hard Copy,* which he set his VCR to record every day, to make sure that Paramount was holding up its end of the deal.

It took only six months for the company to break its word by allowing *Hard Copy,* on September 23, to air a half-minute clip of Clooney and Balitran on the set of *Batman and Robin.* The footage, taken by a paparazzo, was innocuous enough, but it was the last straw as far as Clooney was concerned. He fired off another letter to Paramount in which he made his feelings crystal clear. The letter read, in part, as follows: "So now we begin. Officially. No interviews from this day on. Nothing from ER, nothing from *One Fine Day,* nothing from *Batman and Robin,* and nothing from DreamWorks' first film, *The Peacemaker.* These interviews will be reserved for all press but you. *Access Hollywood, E!,* whoever." Clooney's terse outburst might sound like a tantrum from a spoiled child, but he believed, rightly, that he had as much right to his privacy as anyone else. If this was what he had to do to preserve that privacy, then so be it.

His only fear was that his latest gesture might be an empty one, that his bold maneuver would be reduced to a display of false bravado if no one else in the community supported him. At the end of the day, after all, ER and the film projects with which he was associated had to look out for themselves. He could hardly expect them to join him in his peremptory boycott. But then, much to his surprise and relief, a number of his Hollywood colleagues gave shows of support. Dean Cain, the star of *Lois and Clark: The New Adventures of Superman*, responded to the news of Clooney's boycott by abruptly canceling a scheduled interview with *Entertainment Tonight*. Even better, Clooney's costars on ER — Anthony Edwards, Laura Innes, Eriq La Salle, Julianna Margulies, Gloria Reuben, Sherry Stringfield, and Noah Wyle — wrote a letter of their own to ET's producers: "Based solely on your association with *Hard Copy*, [we] will no longer be participating with you in any form. We have no animosity toward you at all. However, we find it very difficult to work with a show and help it earn money while the company that owns it uses that very same money to purchase paparazzi videos of us for *Hard Copy*."

Clooney may have had misgivings about how his actions would be perceived in Hollywood, but he told the *L.A. Times* that, the way he saw things, "I'm not punching anybody and I'm not suing anybody. If it works and there's some change, great. If it doesn't, I did it to take a stand." Much to his delight, changes did begin to take effect, no doubt hastened along when word reached Paramount of the impressive list of stars who were pledging their support for Clooney's crusade: Rosie O'Donnell, Madonna, Jim Carrey, Ellen DeGeneres, Tom Cruise, and Steven Spielberg were among the Hollywood heavyweights who demanded changes in the way the tabloid shows did business. The megacorporation agreed it would no longer purchase

Ellen Degeneres plants one on Clooney

GREGG DEGUIRE / LONDON FEATURES

video footage of celebrities' children or tape shot by anyone instigating a confrontation with a celebrity. Clooney wanted more — "What they should have said is they wouldn't buy any more paparazzi video" — but he had to admit he'd gotten a lot more out of Paramount than he'd ever thought possible. What's more, as he tells *George*, he was happy that he'd only started the ball rolling by responding to the fact that *Hard Copy* had broken its word by airing an "innocuous story. It was a picture of me and my girlfriend. It wasn't some story about me screwing a sheep."

This remark demonstrates Clooney's ability to maintain his sense of humor during his fight with the tabloids, but he has also remained painfully aware, from the very moment he began his campaign, that his battle is a serious one. His greatest fear, from the beginning, has been that someone would be hurt in a confrontation with the paparazzi who hunt down the footage so highly prized by the tabloid shows. And yes, there had been injuries already — albeit mostly to photographers who had run afoul of Sean Penn, Woody Harrelson, and Alec Baldwin and had received shiners and mangled cameras for their trouble. But more frightening to him were the occasions on which only dumb luck had prevented someone from being very seriously wounded. There was, for example, the day that Arnold Schwarzenegger, returning from the hospital with his wife and young children, was run off the road by a paparazzi pursuit team. This sort of incident convinced Clooney that the stakes were higher than anyone had thought, that it was open season on celebrities and the hunt was on. He told as much to Oprah Winfrey while promoting *Batman and Robin* on her daily talk show: "At some point there has to be a certain responsibility, because when a tabloid show will offer $300,000 for a picture of Madonna's baby, that's a bounty hunter is what you create, and what happens is you have people kicking in front doors of people's homes to get shots, and that's the danger."

The danger became all too real in the last days of August 1997, when most of North America had Saturday-night television shows interrupted by a brief news bulletin informing them that Diana, Princess of Wales, had been injured in a car accident in Paris. The details were sketchy at first — early reports said she had suffered undisclosed injuries, which were soon said to include broken arms and a serious leg wound — but within a few hours, just after midnight Eastern Standard Time, the story developed to its horrifying conclusion: Princess Di had passed away. By the following morning, rumors that paparazzi had been chasing her chauffeured Mercedes Benz through the streets of Paris in the moments leading up to the crash were confirmed. Diana — who takes her name, ironically, from the Greek goddess of the hunt — had been hunted down and killed by the paparazzi who had stalked her for her entire adult life.

Clooney's worst fears had been realized, and in the flurry of activity following Princess Di's death he was asked by friends, colleagues, and news reporters to comment on the tragic events. On September 3, he held a press conference at which he lashed out at the tabloid media with unprecedented anger, calling the purveyors of tabloid "news" the journalistic equivalent of crack dealers who should be punished for supplying their print and video drugs to addicts. He reserved his harshest remarks for Steven Coz, editor of the *National Enquirer* and self-appointed defender of the tabloids, which now found themselves under attack from all directions. Clooney wondered aloud how Coz and his colleagues could sleep at night and summed up his argument with four simple words: "You should be ashamed."

But before he wound up his comments, Clooney hinted at the strategy he would adopt to fight tabloid journalism. His boycott had been effective enough, but he wanted to help make more widespread changes. He had, for a few months now, been meeting with his Hollywood colleagues to discuss ways to go about approaching the U.S. Supreme Court to amend libel laws and make it more difficult for the tabloids to buy stories or footage obtained through illegal means. He made his plans clearer in the September 3 press conference, telling the world that, if the biggest legal barrier to going after tabloids and paparazzi was the practical impossibility of establishing "malicious intent," as required by law in order to prove liability on the part of journalists or photographers, then those were "two words in the law that I will spend every free moment trying to change." His boycott of *Entertainment Tonight*, by comparison, was small potatoes.

Predictably, there was some fallout from his candid comments. Three weeks later, when he attended the premiere of *The Peacemaker* with girlfriend Celine Balitran, the paparazzi gathered outside the theater refused to take his picture. Some of the idiots even heckled him.

Clooney didn't seem too upset.

SEVEN

LOVE, MARRIAGE, AND BEYOND

Long before Clooney declared them public enemy number one, the tabloids had been thoroughly frustrated by his willingness to speak candidly about whatever happened to be on his mind at the moment. Going after them with well-timed verbal assaults at press conferences and in magazine and television interviews added insult to the injury they already felt he had done to them by refusing to leave any skeletons in his closet for them to find. Not exactly grounds for righteous indignation in the real world, but no one has ever claimed that tabloid staffers are necessarily human. Try as they might, the tabloids couldn't come up with anything juicy on Clooney because he'd already admitted his wild past to anyone who bothered to ask him about it. Why deny it? As he told GQ, he wouldn't mind doing an anti-drug commercial as long as he could just be straight about it: "You know what, guys? I grew up in the 70s. I did some drugs along the way. Didn't have a huge problem ever, was never addicted, but I did them like most everyone that was

around me did then . . . and let me give you the
shortcut: It isn't worth it, it's pretty much useless, and
for the most part I would recommend that you don't
do it." His philosophy was simple. If he just let everyone know about his storied past as though it were no
big deal, it never would be.

The best the tabloids have been able to do in recent
years is to report that any woman Clooney has been
spotted with, whether she be Courtney Cox or Cindy
Crawford, is his latest conquest. So bizarre are some
of their stories — one claimed that he and Madonna
were an item shortly after the birth of her daughter
— it's a wonder they haven't accused him of being
romantically involved with his Aunt Rosemary during
the time he stayed with her. Clooney isn't shy about
his past, but concedes, almost sadly, that he's not the
ladies' man everyone makes him out to be, or at least
isn't one anymore: "If I was going out with one tenth
of the girls I get accused of," he tells *Biography*, "I
wouldn't have time to do anything." Anyone who's
taken a glance at his hectic production schedule won't
have any trouble believing this claim. But don't
assume that George has gathered up his toys and
now locks himself away in his Hollywood Hills home,
safe from fun and excitement. Clooney does, as he
assures his fans in an *Us* interview, "absolutely know
how to have a good time." Just ask any of his recently
divorced housemates, who cavort around his house
with him, playing foosball and reminding him of the
joys of bachelorhood.

Clooney hasn't always been a bachelor, though. In
1984, while he was acting in a small local play, he
met a pretty young actress named Talia Balsam, who
also appeared in the play. She wasn't a great actress
— although she did land a role in the 1985 made-for-

television movie *Consenting Adults* — but she did have some talent. More importantly, she seemed to understand Clooney and his weird sense of humor. She was a lot of fun, and they had a fun relationship for a while, but she left him. "It broke his heart," says Richard Kind, one of Clooney's close friends and a star on *Mad about You* and *Spin City*, in an interview with *People Online*. Clooney and Balsam eventually got back together and in 1989 packed up a Winnebago and drove to Las Vegas, where they were married at the White Lace and Promises Chapel. It was just the kind of wedding Clooney's friends would have predicted, had they been able to predict that their free-spirited bachelor friend would ever consent to tie the knot.

Unfortunately, the marriage lasted only slightly longer than the honeymoon. After three years of brief ups and seemingly interminable downs, Clooney and Balsam agreed that they should put an end to their marital charade and file for divorce. They officially split in 1992, with Clooney admitting to *Vanity Fair* that he "probably — *definitely* — wasn't someone who should have been married at that point." Their breakup was, according to Clooney, hardly acrimonious. The fact that he took full responsibility for their marriage's failure certainly helped: "We'd get into a fight and I'd just mentally leave," he admits in an *Us* interview. "I'd think, 'In a relationship, we should never have this kind of a fight.' Then, instead of figuring out how to make it work, I looked for a way to get out of it. The truth is, you shouldn't be married if you're that kind of person." Good advice for anyone anxious to run off and turn a Vegas vacation into an impromptu wedding ceremony.

To tell the truth, however, Clooney should have realized long before he ran off to get married to Talia

Balsam that his spontaneous commitments to women would never do him much good. This is the man, after all, who not long before marrying Balsam decided to move in with Kelly Preston, who is currently married to John Travolta. That in itself does not necessarily demonstrate poor judgment. Lots of men in their mid-twenties have "lived in sin," as it used to be called, with beautiful women. But not many of them have decided to do so after their *first* date with the woman in question, and that's precisely what Clooney did. He claims to have learned his lesson, but doesn't say whether he did so before or after he tied the knot. He tells the *Us* journalist, "I'm much more cautious than I ever was before. I was always Mr. Full-On Spontaneous. I was like, 'Let's go! Whatever you want, let's do it.' Then, as you get a bit older, you start to go, 'You know what? Maybe we should go out a little bit first.'" Although he admits the experience made him start to think more seriously about allowing some time to think things over before taking yet another leap of faith into a relationship, he doesn't regret his brief cohabitation with Preston at all.

And how could he, really? If it weren't for his relationship with her, he would never have met the love of his life, the companion who moved in with him soon after he moved out of Preston's apartment and has stuck with him through thick and thin ever since. No, Clooney didn't shack up with another woman; he merely took custody of the black potbellied pig, Max, that he had given Preston as a birthday gift. Potbellied pigs aren't huge animals — they weigh approximately 125 pounds on average — but Max was 150 pounds of pork that Preston couldn't handle on her own. She and Clooney had parted amicably, so she didn't really like the idea of telling people that every time she looked at the pig she thought of her ex-boyfriend.

Caring for a potbellied pig, a breed that hails from the jungles of China and Vietnam, is a time-consuming endeavor. They can live as long as 18 years, and require daily brushings, hoof and tusk clippings, and plenty of food. They *are* pigs, after all. Because they shed most of their hair in the summer, they are also very susceptible to sunburn, and although greasing up a pig might be some people's idea of fun, it sure wasn't Kelly Preston's. So Clooney took Max in, and now houses him in a custom-made pighouse in his backyard. And Max isn't just a boring lump of ham. More intelligent, presumably, than your average hog, Max has scared an uninvited photographer off Clooney's property, chasing him over a fence and causing him to break his camera in the process. He's also handy at delivering messages, as Clooney's housemates have proved by gently scratching notes such as "Matt, get milk" in the dry skin on his back. More expensive than a Post-it note, but a lot harder to miss.

What's most surprising about Max, perhaps, is that he hasn't figured prominently in any of the tabloid stories about Clooney, although his owner recalls, in a *Hollywood Confidential* piece, the following story about what happened to him and Max during the 1994 L.A. earthquake and muses about what the tabloids might have made of it: "Max was in bed with me and woke up minutes before [the earthquake] happened. And I was yelling at him for waking me up — when everything just exploded. So I'm naked, with Max, and running . . . 'cause I'm in a house on a hill, and if it's going down I want to be up on the street, dodging the next house. My buddy, who lives in the downstairs guest house, comes running up. And he's naked. With a gun, because he thought someone was breaking in. And I'm trying to write a note to my folks, trying to explain to them in case we die that it's not what it seems: two naked men, a gun, and a pig." Quite a picture, even if it does sound like the title for the next Steve Guttenberg movie.

As much as Clooney loves Max — and make no mistake, he's quite attached to his porcine companion — he has finally, after a series of brief flings following his divorce, allowed a flesh-and-blood woman into his life on a regular basis. He met young Celine Balitran, a 25-year-old law student who is a volunteer kindergarten teacher and barroom waitress, in France while visiting a friend at his farmhouse in the countryside just outside Paris. Her fresh features, glowing smile, and sexy French accent entranced Clooney from the moment he saw her, and he soon found himself making small excursions from the set of *The Peacemaker*, which was filming in eastern Europe, to see her in France. When he returned to the United States, he continued courting her via AT&T, and it's a good thing he was making some serious dough by then, because his long-distance bills were outrageous. Within a few months, he had convinced her to visit him in America, he tells *Tribute*, and shortly after she arrived he simply suggested, in his homespun way, that "We should be going out, we should be seeing each other." She agreed, and they've been doing so ever since.

One thing Balitran hadn't known, however, before she started seeing Clooney was that he was a big-time Hollywood star. She knew he was an actor, but had no idea that he was, as Clooney would say, a member of the famous club. That she was able to cope with the mad crush of the fans and media who surrounded her and Clooney wherever they went is a credit to her

Clooney and Celine Balitran
RON DAVIS / SHOOTING STAR

character and clear evidence of her affection for George, but it has also led some to assume, rightly or wrongly, that their relationship is very serious, and even that wedding bells might be heard in the near future. Balitran has not commented on these speculations, but Clooney, although he is careful not to come right out and say he has no plans to marry her, does make a convincing case for his reluctance to tie the knot again in his lifetime. "I've been married before," he tells Oprah Winfrey. "I don't think I was very good at it. I just don't want to do that anymore." But before doing cartwheels, female fans who rejoice that Clooney won't be marrying Balitran need to do a reality check and keep in mind that he won't be marrying *them* anytime soon either.

As if to confirm his new vow against matrimony, Clooney has allowed his home to become not just any old bachelor pad, but a veritable shrine in honor of the sacred covenant of single life. On his living room mantel rests a small statue on which all of his divorced pals have hung their wedding rings after promising never to wear one again. Whether Balitran finds this amusing or disconcerting isn't known for sure, but she can hardly find it reassuring, *Tribute* reports, when Clooney says, "The wedding? We'll hold off on that, thanks. The pig has to die first, you know, and they live for 30 years." If she does hope to marry Clooney, she's apparently in for a good long wait.

Much of Clooney's reluctance to remarry stems from his belief, as espoused on *Prime Time Live*, that "that's when you'd get married . . . if you wanted to have children." And if Clooney seems gun-shy about marriage in general, don't even get him started on raising kids. He had a good childhood, with kind, decent parents who loved and supported him, but doubts he has what it takes to live up to the example set by his own mother and father. Furthermore, he doesn't believe it's fair to risk a child's happiness just to see if he could be a good father: "I just think that kids are the ultimate responsibility," he confides to *Tribute*, "and unless it's something that you absolutely have a burning desire to do, I don't feel you should do it half-assed. And I don't feel like messing anybody's life up, you know?" Or, as he said on *Prime Time Live*, "I need parents, is what I need. I'm looking to be adopted."

Clooney's friends, however, remain unconvinced by his anti-parenting bravado. Nicole Kidman and Michelle Pfeiffer, who've seen him play Uncle George with kids on the set of *One Fine Day* and *The Peace-maker*, aren't buying his routine for a minute. So sure are they he'll be a father before too long — Pfeiffer even goes so far as to tell *Biography*, "Once he gets started [having kids], he'll have 12" — that the two actresses have put up $10,000 apiece in a bet with Clooney that he'll be a father before he turns 40. But Clooney dismisses their chances of collecting on that bet with his characteristically evil wit in his *Tribute* interview: "Yeah, no way am I going to lose any money on this one, because I figure, here's the deal — I get a vasectomy for five grand and I'm up 15 grand right there. I can make a profit." Not that he needs the money, but the pot would keep Max in Purina pot-bellied pig feed for the rest of his life.

Meanwhile, Clooney is as happy as a pig in . . . well, you know. He's still helping ER kill the competition in the weekly ratings wars, has numerous film projects lined up, shares his time with a drop-dead gorgeous girlfriend, and, despite the predictions of the doom-sayers, survived his Batman experience with his career and his sanity intact. How much happier could having a wife and children really make him at this point?

Clooney considers all the options
FOX / SHOOTING STAR

Then again, perhaps the final word on the matter should belong to cousin Miguel Ferrer, who knows Clooney better than anyone. "You know, George likes to come off like Scrooge," he tells *Us* magazine. "Like, 'I fucking hate kids.' And it's just not true. He doesn't hate kids; he's wonderful with them. And I'll tell you, he's been with his present girlfriend, who is so great and unaffected, for a long time, longer than anyone George has ever been with, outside of his wife. After George's divorce, he swore, 'I will *never* get married, I will *never* have kids. But you never know where life is going to take you. I think George may surprise himself.''

Judging from the success he's had since his humble beginnings in small-town Kentucky, Clooney already has.

NOTHING BUT NET: A USER'S GUIDE TO INTERNET RESOURCES FOR GEORGE CLOONEY AND *ER*

Ever since ER hit the air in 1994, its fans have been hitting their computer keyboards and churning out home page after home page of user-friendly information on the show and its stars. Biographies and suitable-for-framing photographs of cast members, gossip, episode synopses, real-time audio and video clips from the show . . . all this and more is available for your inspection. All you need is a modem and a decent Internet server.

But the constant proliferation of ER-related sites makes it nearly impossible for the novice Net surfer, or even the discerning veteran of the information highway, to know where to turn for the best and most reliable sites. Following endless links in search of the best pages is time- and money-consuming, and a hit-and-miss proposition at best.

Tell this to George Clooney, and he'd reply that although he doesn't know much about the Internet — despite the fact that there are well over 100 sites devoted to him — he imagines that it's a lot like basketball. You take your shots at the net; sometimes you score, and sometimes you miss. With this in mind, the following Internet sites on Clooney and ER are rated in terms of basketball scoring.

The very best are issued three-pointers (🏀 🏀 🏀), the solid entries are given a deuce (🏀 🏀), the barely adequate are awarded a foul shot (🏀), and the ones that do nothing but move through dead air are deemed bricks (🧱). Just aim your browser and fire — but caveat surfer: web sites are much less permanent than the printed word, so what's here today may be gone tomorrow.

SITES DEVOTED TO GEORGE CLOONEY

All You Want to Know about George Clooney 🏀 🏀
www.geocities.com/Hollywood/7084/

If you'd like reassurance that some of the people constructing home pages out there actually do have a basic command of the English language, take a shot at this site. It features a very complete Clooney filmography and the best-written brief bio of the star you're likely to find on the Net. Complaints? Well, given the good writing, this home page is long on facts but unfortunately short on text. Still a good bet.

Another George Clooney Page ⓓ
members.aol.com/pfeiffero2/clooney.html

The title of this one says it all: a rather ho-hum site that offers a Batman-heavy collection of photographs and not much else of interest. But the photos are quite attractive, so caped crusader fans may want to check this out.

Baby Bop's George Clooney Page ⓓ ⓓ
members.aol.com./BbyBp/ERClooney.html

Don't worry, this site isn't tended to by Barney's annoying sidekick. Yes, this is a fairly simple page, but simplicity is a virtue here. Instead of the usual hodgepodge of links from text and images, this is a nicely laid-out page, making it easy to find the photos, up-to-date Clooney movie news, and numerous good ER links that are the backbone of the site. Don't leave without reading the quirky Clooney anecdotes, which are hilarious.

Casa de Clooney ⓓ
members.aol.com/InScrubs/index.html

If it's a session of slack-jawed staring at pictures of gorgeous George you're looking for, this is the site for you, the "real Clooniac." Some text would make this a much better page than it is, because no matter what your mother told you, pictures aren't always worth a thousand words. The site's evidence that Clooney is intelligent? A photo. That he has a good sense of humor? Another photo. That he's taken on the tabloids? Yet another photo. Stay for the very quick "Six Degrees of George Clooney" link, but please leave before getting sucked into the "why I lust after George" room.

CelebSite: George Clooney ◀
www.celebsite.com/people/georgeclooney/index.html

This *People*-run site includes a biography and searchable Clooney index, but how much faith can you put in a source that spells Clooney's girlfriend's name wrong? It's Balitran, not Balidran. Jeepers creepers.

Gorgeous George Clooney's Home Page ⑩
www.geocities.com/Hollywood/Lot/1814/

There's not much more here than meets the eye, but the photographs accompanying the biography are first-rate. This one's worth looking at, but don't bother book-marking it.

Ida Kern's Clooney Fan Home Page ⑩ ⑩ ⑩
www.geocities.com/TelevisionCity/4967/

This is an absolutely wonderful site. Apart from the daily updates on Clooney news and the usual bios, filmographies, interview transcripts, and links to ER's theme song, there are also a number of reproductions of autographed Clooney photos and submissions from regular people who've had close encounters with Clooney. Neato. A nice, well-planned, and attractive page that you owe it to yourself to go through from top to bottom. If you don't like this one, you don't like Clooney.

Julie's George Clooney Page ⑩ ⑩
www.geocities.com/Hollywood/2766/
gc1000.htm#oben

There's a veritable gold mine of Clooney stuff here, including Quicktime and AVI video trailers from his movies, soundbites from interviews, and some very nicely reproduced photos of everybody's favorite ER hunk.

Lesley's George Clooney Page ⑩
www.avana.net/~grunt

The owner of this home page means well, loading it with plenty of good photos and up-to-the-minute media buzz about Clooney, but many surfers will wipe out while trying to decipher the spelling-mistake-riddled text. You'll find the complete transcript of Clooney's press conference on paparazzi following Princess Diana's untimely death, for instance, but will have to fight to make sense of it. With a little proofreading, this could be a high-caliber site.

Looney for Clooney Ⓘ
**www.geocities.com/Hollywood/3526/
index.html**

Not the most spectacular site around, but this one is nice to look at and is a reliable jumping-off point to the George Clooney Webring, which is run by the owner of this page. That alone makes it worth a bookmark.

Looney for Clooney ◢
**www.angelfire.com/md/CoxyBrown/
clooney.html**

Not to be confused with the other "Looney for Clooney" site (see above), this page is mainly a tribute to the misuse of the exclamation point (!) and the utter impossibility of using hip-hop lingo to say anything intelligent. It's nice to know that Clooney and his movies are "phat" and "da booomb," but what the hell does that mean? Downloading a virus might be more fun.

Marty's George Clooney Page Ⓘ
**copper.ucs.indiana.edu/~mtsai/
george_clooney.html**

Before you get too excited about entering Martin Tsai's gallery of Clooney photos from his "private collection," here's the bad news: you've seen them all before. The pictures are nice enough, and Marty does provide some handy links to other sights, but this site is a yawner otherwise.

Naomi's Clooney Crazy Page ◢
**www.geocities.com/Hollywood/Set/7870/
clooney.html**

Previously known best for reminding us that wRiTiNg In AlTeRnAtInG lOwErCaSe aNd CaPiTaL lEtTeRs Is aNnOyInG (see?), this site has traded that vice for another: the dreaded exclamation point. Naomi joins the owner of the hip-hop "Looney for Clooney" site in her belief that exuberant punctuation is the sincerest form of flattery. Or maybe it's just a not-so-subtle way of trying to make us believe that *One Fine Day* really is "the best movie ever!"

This hokey, juvenile site does provide some nice Clooney photos, but since most are magazine covers you probably already own, why waste your time here? Or, as Naomi might put it, don't waste your time here!

SITES DEVOTED TO *ER*

Adam Barth's ER *Page* ⓘⓘ
members.aol.com/Head26/index.htm

This is a very good site indeed. Mr. Barth doesn't just include the usual bios of the main cast, he also provides information on the supporting actors and characters. Go here for spoilers on upcoming episodes — but don't worry, you'll have plenty of advance warning if you wish to avoid them — or for brief episode synopses if you missed the first dozen episodes of the show and can't wait for Scott Hollifield (see below) to get around to summarizing them. Only one thing keeps this from being a top-notch home page: the white text on a gray marble background can be tough to read.

Danny's ER *Page* ⓘⓘⓘ
www.seas.gwu.edu:80/student/danny/er

This page is ranked within the top five percent of all sites — and with good reason. This is a startlingly attractive page with a nice layout, sensible organization (your first link here is to an ER FAQ), and an insane amount of information on the show. The oddities section is particularly worth checking out: Did you know that Clooney's lines are dubbed into Italian by Fabrizio Temperini? Bookmark immediately.

Debbie's ER *Page* ⓘ
www.cas.usf.edu/lis/lis2002/spring96/ sellerd.html

This site, comprised mainly of links to other, better, home pages, is out of date — Sherry Stringfield still graces its introductory photo, and Laura Innex is nowhere to be seen — but it's a nicely organized primer on the show and its stars.

ER Live ⓘ ⓘ

www.erline.com.main.html

Stay far away from this page if you find it irritating to wait for advertisements to download from the Net. But if you can get by this (keep in mind, after all, that the site is operated by NBC and Warner Bros., and probably not out of the goodness of their corporate hearts), then you're in for a real treat. You'll find gobs of information on the show here, including chat transcripts and RealVideo interviews regarding the fourth season's live premiere, and even a trivia challenge. If you believe in capitalism, take a gander.

ER Online Compendium ⓘ ⓘ ⓘ

www.fix.net/~will/er/

As its name might suggest, this site is as thorough as can be. You'll be serenaded by the ER theme as you browse through the compendium's many pages of news, interview transcripts, magazine articles, and cast bios — there's even one for Glenne Headly, who played pediatric surgeon Abby Keaton on the show. Attractive, massive, and thoroughly impressive, the compendium is also easy to navigate and includes — wonder of wonders for an ER Web site — good material originally written for the site itself. Stop reading and turn on your modem.

Gonzo's Emergency Room Website ⓘ ⓘ

www.euphora.com/gonzo

An attractive site for people who wish to brush up on their foreign-language skills; this one is German-English bilingual. Gonzo dredges up the usual cast bios, but also includes pages on the show's production staff and writers — a very nice touch. Go here for a link to watch ER live on the Net if that sort of thing interests you.

John Callaghan's ER Page ⓘ

ng.simplenet.com/er/

An otherwise strong site is marred by some trashy material. Skip the many bad ER fan fictions here and take the rumors section with a huge grain of salt. Do you really believe that

George Clooney has recently had a nose job? Do you really care that the cast of the show had a nice time at lunch together a couple of weeks ago? No, probably not. Neatest feature: a clock that counts down the seconds until the next broadcast of the show. Bookmark this site, but don't open all its doors.

Love in Scrubs ① ①
monet.xoom.com/scrubs/

This user-friendly site is the Internet equivalent of group therapy for people who are obsessed with network television programs and their stars. Heavily weighted toward Clooney worship, this is the place to go to let loose all that pent-up estrogen and let the world know why you love your favorite ER star. You can sign up to receive the Love in Scrubs newsletter, have on-line chats, and even join an e-mail discussion group dedicated to your psychosis. It beats stalking, I guess.

NBC's Official ER Page ① ①
www.nbc.com/tvcentral/shows/er/index.html

This is the site from which many others crib the cast bios, character sketches, photos, and other items of interest you've been reading all along. It's worth checking out, and will lead those anxious to part with their greenbacks to plenty of official ER merchandise, but it's left in the dust by most amateur home pages. Imagine going to the official site for the show and not being able to find any information on William H. Macy. Unbelievable!

Scott Hollifield's ER Page ① ① ①
alt.TV.ER

Scott Hollifield's oft-relocated page grants him the title of ER Web king. The presentation is beautiful. The episode synopses, which include a summary of medical procedures performed on the show, are incredibly detailed, and his reviews of them are intelligent and to the point. Even more incredibly, he writes them immediately following each new broadcast. The usual stuff is here too — links to cast bios, filmographies, FAQs, et cetera — but you'll want to bookmark this page for the synopses alone. Hollifield is a Web workhorse par excellence.

SITES DEVOTED TO OTHER STARS OF *ER*

I Love Sherry Stringfield ⓧ ⓧ
www.geocities.com/TelevisionCity/1737/index.html

Absence makes the heart grow fonder, as is apparent from this site devoted to the many charms of Dr. Susan Lewis, which is still updated regularly. Then again, by the time you get this slow-loading lovefest on your computer screen in its entirety, Stringfield is likely to have her own sitcom on CBS.

Julianna Margulies Devotion Center ⓧ ⓧ
www.Kentoday.demon.co.uk/jmdc/

The JMDC, as it's affectionately known, does for men what Love in Scrubs does for women, but in nowhere near the same depth. Still, this nice little page, which includes a CNN RealVideo interview with Margulies, is worth a look.

Laura Innes Fan Page ⓧ ⓧ
www.geocities.com/Hollywood/Academy/5999/

This is a nice, straightforward page devoted to the nasty Dr. Kerry Weaver and the actress who plays her. It's quite unspectacular — who'da thunk there'd even be a page devoted to her? — but if you want to know more about Innes and her long Hollywood career, this is the page to go to.

Nothing but Noah Wyle ⓧ ⓧ ⓧ
www.geocities.com/Hollywood/Lot/7838

Don't come knocking on this site's door if all you're after is a chance to moon over Wyle. Much to its credit, this home page is devoted solely to Wyle's professional career, and leaves his personal life untouched in favor of audio and video clips concerning his life as a performer. Nevertheless, the dark, sensuous photos here should be enough to keep Wyle fans happy. A beautiful site.

The Official Abraham Benrubi Page ⑩ ⑩
www.csh.rit.edu/~phbob/benrubi.html

Fans of Jerry unite! This page is devoted to the wit and questionable wisdom of ER's resident lunkhead. But it does raise one question: How can it be that there is a home page devoted to Abraham Benrubi, but none for Eriq La Salle?

Wendy's Anthony Edwards Page ⑩ ⑩
www.geocities.com/Hollywood/7542/

Point your way here to enter the Anthony Edwards lookalike contest. Fortunately, this isn't just another soppy ER love-in. What you'll find here are nice photographs of Edwards in casual poses and basic information on his life and career.

Clooney and Celine Balitran

Clooney and Karen Duffy

Clooney and Max

First Annual Breakthrough Awards Party:
Clooney, Jason Priestley, Grant Shon

GREGG DEGUIRE / LONDON FEATURES

Premiere of Rosie O'Donnell Show, 10 June 96
with Susan Lucci and Rosie O'Donnell

AP / WIDE WORLD PHOTOS

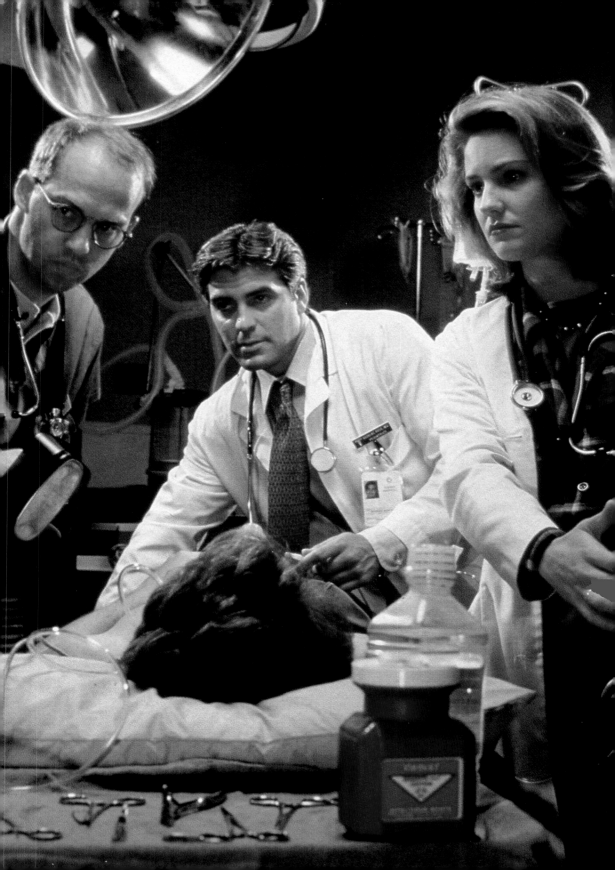

Nick, Rosemary, and George Clooney

Clooney and Michelle Pfeiffer

ALL ABOUT *ER*: A VIEWER'S GUIDE TO THE SHOW

The most popular program on network television is the brainchild of Michael Crichton, a 55-year-old native Chicagoan with a degree from prestigious Harvard Medical School. Crichton based the series on his personal experiences as a student at Massachusetts General Hospital and pitched the idea to NBC, which subsequently developed the program in association with Constant c Productions, Amblin Entertainment, and Warner Bros. Television.

As NBC's lengthy run as the top-rated U.S. network suggests, NBC executives recognize a sure thing when they see one, and Crichton's concept looked golden. He had already demonstrated his Midas touch as the best-selling author of novels such as *The Andromeda Strain*, *Congo*, and, of course, *Jurassic Park*, which became the second-highest-grossing film of all time under the direction of Steven Spielberg, and now it was television's turn to reap some of the very considerable benefits of a partnership with Crichton.

The two-hour pilot episode, "24 Hours," was written by Crichton and aired on September 19, 1994. Word that the new show would join perennial ratings champion *Seinfeld* on the Thursday-night schedule had been intended to ensure a few weeks' worth of steady viewership no matter how the show might be initially received. But it was

Cast of ER (third season)
WARNER BROS. / SHOOTING STAR

immediately apparent that this was a show that could stand on its own two feet. Those fortunate enough to have believed all the pre-season hype and tuned in for the premiere were treated to a viewing experience unlike any they'd had before.

The show may have looked like any other medical drama at first blush, but it became clear before long that something very different was going on here. This was a case of *St. Elsewhere* meets *Rambo*, a flying-by-the-seat-of-its-pants romp through the palpable frenzy of an inner-city emergency room that wasn't shy about showing the bloody side of the profession and took the bold step of developing its characters not only through their interactions, but also through non-stop action the likes of which prime time had never seen.

"Traditional medical shows are really about the patients," says Co-Executive Producer John Wells in describing what sets ER apart from other shows. "Our series is about physicians." This emphasis on characterization keeps the large stable of writers busy and mitigates the minor lapses in medical realism that occasionally creep into the show for the sake of dramatic license. It's not that the show plays fast and loose with the medical facts — a number of nurses assist Lance Gentile as consultants, ensuring that the medicine never gets too wacky — but if ER were a perfectly accurate re-creation of a hospital emergency room, its characters would spend most of their time waiting for lab results and stitching minor lacerations.

Luckily, they don't. The fictional staff of Cook County General Hospital in Chicago — based on the actual Chicago hospital of the same name — is much too busy dealing with the life-and-death cases that stream into the ER at an incredible rate and trying to dedicate themselves to their profession while facing monumental personal challenges of their own. Putting a production of this technical and narrative complexity together requires a lot of work on the part of cast and crew, who spend long hours shooting the bulk of the show's scenes in Los Angeles and going to Chicago six or seven times per year for exterior shots.

The hard work has paid off. In its first season, ER was nominated for 23 Emmys, winning eight, and was awarded the Emmy for Outstanding Drama Series in its second season. By its third season, for which it was awarded the Screen Actors Guild Award for Outstanding Ensemble Performance in a Drama Series, the show had put a stranglehold on the Neilsen ratings, becoming the highest-rated show on television. It commonly attracts more than 40 percent of the viewing audience for its time slot, and remains a favorite of critics and casual viewers alike.

CBS, which originally placed its own entry in the medical-drama sweepstakes, the more quirky and dark-humored *Chicago Hope*, into the same time slot as ER, quickly backed off and moved the show to Monday night. ABC mounted a challenge with *Murder One* in season number two, but this show was disposed of in short order, leaving the NBC series as the undisputed champion of the network ratings wars in its second and third seasons. But despite its big ratings numbers, the show does not make any money for the network and its producers. In fact, all the advertising revenue in the world couldn't hope to cover the escalating salaries of the show's stars. It's a little-known fact that the show actually loses money each week. But its producers are hardly crying poor: once the show enters syndication — which should happen within the next two years — they'll be laughing all the way to the bank.

With its myriad story lines and ceaselessly shifting action, ER relies on a stable of fine actors who must be able to work within the ensemble and move beyond it as the script dictates. As was pointed out in an early *Entertainment Weekly* story on the show, "it takes a lot more than fast action and true-to-life-and-death dialogue to keep people coming back. What really brings the blood, sweat, and sutures to life are the six actors that work ER's corridors." Most of them have numerous stage and screen appearances to their credit, and all of them put in 14-hour days on the set to create these compelling characters.

THE MAJOR CHARACTERS

Dr. Peter Benton (Eriq La Salle) is a self-righteous surgical resident who has been Dr. John Carter's mentor and agitator since the series premiere. A gifted surgeon who adheres to a strict moral code (except when he engages in adultery with Jeanie Boulet), he demands professionalism and perfection from everyone at Cook County General, himself most of all.

Jeanie Boulet (Gloria Reuben), compassionate Physician Assistant and former love interest of Peter Benton, becomes a major presence on ER late in the first season in "Love among the Ruins." Having contracted HIV from her philandering husband, she struggles to put her professional and personal lives back in order while dealing with her disease.

Dr. John Carter (Noah Wyle) is responsible for innocence and idealism in the ER, though he has learned, in his progress from meek med student to sub-intern to surgical resident under Dr. Benton's tutelage, to temper his overzealous dedication to patient care with just a dash of necessary cynicism.

Dr. Mark Greene (Anthony Edwards) is the show's ultra-competent pivotal character. Forced to choose between marriage and career, he juggles his responsibilities to County's patients, staff, and administration as ER Attending Physician while pining for Susan Lewis and trying to piece his fragmented life back together.

Carol Hathaway (Julianna Margulies) very nearly didn't make it past the pilot episode, in which she attempted suicide. Bowing to the wishes of ER's test audiences, the show's producers resurrected her as the uncompromising head nurse in the ER and continue to tease viewers

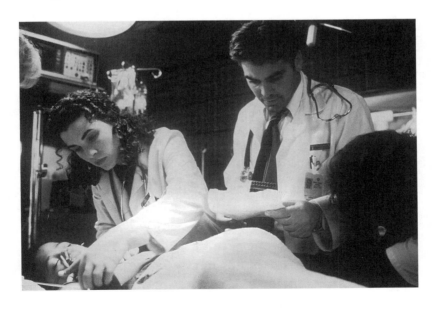

Clooney and Julianna Margulies a.k.a. Nurse Hathaway

WARNER BROS. / AP/WORLD WIDE PHOTOS

who would really like her and Doug to cut the crap and just get married.

Dr. Susan Lewis (Sherry Stringfield), Resident Physician, left Chicago for Phoenix in the show's third season ("Union Station") after deciding she needed to do something more with her life than try to manage the chaos in the ER. Her departure puts an end to any hope that she and Mark Greene will become romantically involved and reunites her with her sister and niece, little Susie.

Dr. Doug Ross (George Clooney) is the brooding Pediatric Emergency Medicine Fellow. He's a womanizing borderline alcoholic whose wholehearted commitment to the children he treats sometimes gets him into trouble, especially when he stubbornly challenges authority in the interest of his own beliefs.

Dr. Kerry Weaver (Laura Innes), Attending Physician, has ruffled feathers in the ER ever since her debut in the season-two premiere ("Welcome Back, Carter"). Her penchant for administrative order wins her many enemies — Susan Lewis chief among them — but she demonstrates her compassionate side in her friendship with Jeanie Boulet.

THE SUPPORTING CAST

No hospital would be able to function without a crack support staff and an assortment of medical and surgical specialists who lend their expertise as circumstances warrant in an emergency room. Similarly, the success of any hospital drama depends nearly as much on its minor players as on its major ones. ER has had the good fortune to employ some of the finest actors in the business in supporting and recurring roles, though it can be difficult to keep track of them all at times.

THE HIGHER-UPS

Dr. Donald Anspaugh (John Aylward)
Chief of Staff

Dr. Neal Bernstein (David Spielburg)
Head of Pediatrics

Dr. Div Cvetic (John Terry)
Psychiatrist and Susan's former boyfriend

Dr. Anna Del Amico (Mario Bello)
Pediatrics resident

Dr. Greg Fischer (Harry I. Lennix)
Infectious diseases specialist

Dr. Angela Hicks (CCH Pounder)
Attending Surgeon

Dr. Jack Kaysen (Sam Anderson)
Cardiologist

Dr. Abby Keaton (Glenne Headly)
Attending Surgeon, Pediatrics

Dr. David Morgenstern (William H. Macy)
Head of Emergency Services

Dr. William Swift (Michael Ironside)
Head of Emergency Services

Dr. John Taglieri (Rick Rossovich)
Staff Orthopedist and Carol's ex-fiancé

Dr. Carl Vucelich (Ron Rifkin)
Vascular Surgeon

THE LOWER-DOWNS

Haleh Adams (Yvette Freeman)
ER Nurse

E-Ray Bozman (Charles Noland)
Nursing Assistant/Administrative Desk Attendant

Deb Chen (Ming-Na Wen)
Medical Student

Dr. Maggie Doyle (Jorjan Fox)
ER *Intern*

Randi Fronczak (Kristin Minter)
Administrative Desk Attendant

Dr. Dennis Gant (Omar Epps)
Surgical Intern

Wendy Goldman (Vanessa Marquez)
ER *Nurse*

Chuny Harquez (Laura Ceron)
ER *Nurse*

Iris (Joanna Gleason)
Infomercial Director

Lily Jarvik (Lily Mariye)
ER *Nurse*

Jerry Markovic (Abraham Benrubi)
Administrative Desk Attendant

Malik McGrath (Deezer D)
ER *Nurse*

Conni Oligaro (Conni Marie Brazelton)
ER *Nurse*

Harper Tracy (Christine Elise)
Medical Student

Lydia Wright (Ellen Crawford)
ER *Nurse*

THE FAMILY MEMBERS

Jackie Benton (Khandi Alexander)
Peter's sister

Mae Benton (Beah Richards)
Peter's mother

Al Boulet (Wolfgang Bodison and Michael Beach)
Jeanie's husband

Jennifer Greene (Christine Harnos)
Mark's wife

Rachel Greene (Yvonne Zima)
Mark's daughter

Helen Hathaway (Rose Gregorio)
Carol's mother

Chloe Lewis (Kathleen Wilholte)
Susan's sister

Cookie Lewis (Valerie Perrine)
Susan's mother

Henry Lewis (Paul Dooley)
Susan's father

Ray Ross (James Farentino)
Doug's father

Mrs. Ross (Piper Laurie)
Doug's mother

Walt (Ving Rhames)
Peter's brother-in-law

THE NOTCHES ON
DOUG'S BEDPOST

Linda Farrell (Andrea Parker)
Pharmaceutical representative

Hulda (Nicole Nagel)
Finnish flight attendant

Karen Hines (Marg Helgenberger)
Ray Ross's business partner

Diane Leeds (Lisa Zane)
Mother of basketball-playing Jake

THE REST

Reilly Brown (Scott Michael Campbell)
Paramedic

Mrs. Cavanaugh/Madame X (Rosemary Clooney)
Torch singer and Alzheimer's patient

Charlie (Kirstin Dunst)
Homeless teen prostitute and friend of Doug

Al Grabarsky (Mike Genovese)
Policeman and Lydia's husband

William Litman (Chris Edwards)
Carol's physics classmate

Raul Melendez (Carlos Gomez)
Paramedic

Carla Reese (Lisa Nicole Carson)
Peter's girlfriend and mother of his child

Raymond "Shep" Shepherd (Ron Eldard)
Paramedic and Carol's former boyfriend

Kathy Snyder (Megan Gallagher)
Legal counsel for County General

Loretta Sweet (Mary Mara)
Cancer-stricken ex-prostitute

A REVIEWER'S DIARY OF *ER*

SEASON ONE

"24 Hours"

Season 1, Episode 1

ORIGINAL AIR DATE: September 19, 1994
WRITTEN BY: Michael Crichton
DIRECTED BY: Rod Holcomb
GRADE: A

This is where it all begins, the two-hour pilot for the fast-paced medical drama about the exciting and tragic events of the emergency room of Cook County General Hospital. Its breakneck speed allows this inaugural episode to bypass the problem that plagues most pilots: awkward character introduction. Fact is, there's just not enough time in this day — or at least in this episode — for characters to pause and introduce themselves and others to the audience in the fawning and mechanical fashion to which we've become accustomed in season premieres. Amid the gore and commotion of the ER, which is breathtakingly and painstakingly depicted here, these characters just seem already to *be*. Michael Crichton and the production team have apparently chosen to let the characters develop through the series action, which seems for now to have been a very good choice indeed.

It will take some time, of course, to discover where these characters come from and where they are headed, and to see how willing the writers are to confront the myriad tough issues revolving around inner-city health care, but if this episode is any indication, ER is likely to be a winner with critics and the public alike. One thing is clear: this is not *St. Elsewhere*. This is a show with attitude and energy to spare. How many shows, for instance, kill off a major character (Nurse Carol Hathaway, who apparently takes a drug overdose) in the very episode in which she and the others are introduced? NBC and its audience are going to be expecting big things from this show, and ER looks like it's willing and able to deliver.

"Day One"

Season 1, Episode 2

ORIGINAL AIR DATE: September 22, 1994
WRITTEN BY: John Wells
DIRECTED BY: Mimi Leder
GRADE: B+

The risk of having aired one of the single most remarkable television pilots in recent memory is that subsequent episodes will not be able to live up to it. Too often, the vast energies expended during the production of a pilot leave cast and crew drained and unable to meet their own high standards. ER has not fallen victim to this tendency. The second episode is deftly acted and shrewdly written. Both of these strengths assert themselves in the story of Dr. Susan Lewis's attempts to find help for an elderly homeless man with psychological problems. She runs up against Dr. Div Cvetic, a psychiatric consult who offers little sympathy to the patient or to Susan's determination to help him, but we soon discover that she and Cvetic are romantically entangled. This isn't exactly a bombshell, but it's a nicely timed revelation that allows the writers to hint that there may be more lurking behind the hospital's other working relationships than first meets the eye.

Meanwhile, Clooney turns in a strong performance as the ER's pediatrics specialist. He throws all the desperation — both physical and psychological — he can muster into his portrayal of Doug Ross's valiant efforts to save an eight-year-old hit-and-run victim. He'll be a character to watch, especially if he continues to make such a personal and emotional investment in his fragile young patients. The other highlight of the episode is the romantic and comedic treatment of Mark Greene and his wife, Jenn. She rushes to the hospital to celebrate with Mark after passing her bar exam, and the two are caught in the act, literally, a short time later. All things considered, a fine second showing.

"Going Home"

Season 1, Episode 3

ORIGINAL AIR DATE: September 29, 1994
WRITTEN BY: Lydia Woodward
DIRECTED BY: Mark Tinker
GRADE: B

The plot thickens. Nurse Carol Hathaway returns to work following her suicide attempt and has to face Doug. It had been vaguely hinted that these two were romantically involved at some point preceding the pilot episode's action, and, although the certainty of this fact remains as murky as the nature of their former relationship, it seems that her attempt on her own life was somehow sparked by fallout from their breakup. Doug, for his part, certainly feels responsible for her near death, and spends the day trying to renew his relationship with her. But, in a highly suspect twist, she reveals that she's seeing Dr. John Taglieri, the staff orthopedist. This plot thread has its strengths and weaknesses. For example, holding some of the facts about Carol and Doug's past relationship in store is a good idea. For now, we know as much as we need to — that Doug is a heavy drinker and a womanizer — and by not putting all the cards on the table the writers ensure they can play another hand if it becomes necessary for dramatic purposes down the road. However, using Taglieri as a romantic roadblock for Doug isn't a very credible maneuver. It's not hard to believe that a person in Carol's fragile emotional state might rebound to someone like him following a breakup, but it is hard to believe that he's so completely oblivious to his own shaky status as her boyfriend. How dense can a doctor be?

The rest of the episode is devoted to Mark's treatment of an entire family marred by domestic violence and to the curious meanderings of a disoriented torch singer known as "Madame X." Fans of George Clooney will be interested to know that this part is played by none other than his aunt, famed vocalist Rosemary Clooney. She does a steady job in the role, but is clearly employed more as a star-powered in-joke than anything else.

"Hit and Run"

Season 1, Episode 4

ORIGINAL AIR DATE: October 6, 1994
WRITTEN BY: Paul Manning
DIRECTED BY: Mimi Leder
GRADE: C+

The crux of this episode is Eriq La Salle's performance as Dr. Peter Benton, who, up to now, has mainly devoted himself to making life a living hell for John Carter, the cute, bumbling medical student under his supervision. La Salle turns up the heat when Benton clashes with another resident who is competing with him for the same fellowship, and delivers a performance consisting of a lot more than just a series of burning looks. Stories like this prove perfect complements to the show's rampant action, reminding viewers that behind the blood and guts of an ER lie the personal concerns and petty jealousies that might be found in any workplace. ER's consistent willingness not just to acknowledge the fact that doctors are neither superhumans nor automatons, but to exploit its dramatic potential, lends it a well-roundedness that's not easy to find on the prime-time schedule.

That being said, this is the show's weakest episode to date — which should be taken more as a compliment to the first three episodes than a condemnation of the fourth. Susan's efforts to diagnose a salesman who won't take the cellular phone away from his ear long enough for her to get any work done is cute, but ultimately empty of much significance. The story of a five-year-old boy with a schizophrenic mother has more potential, but proves itself before long to be little more than a transparent mechanism for arranging an opportunity for Doug and Carol to work together. The most promising material here concerns Mark, who handles two heart patients while anticipating Jenn's five-day departure for work. We've seen Mark walk confidently through the world of the strictly professional; now it's time to see him negotiate an even trickier terrain, trying to hold his job and marriage together while his wife does the same. With ER's writers at the helm, this is bound to lead to a compelling story.

"Into That Good Night"

Season 1, Episode 5

ORIGINAL AIR DATE: October 13, 1994
WRITTEN BY: Robert Nathan
DIRECTED BY: Charles Haid
GRADE: B+

Doug's doings in this episode lead one to pose a question of ER that might better be asked of U.S. health-care professionals and management in general. He once again becomes personally involved in the life of one of his patients when he's confronted with the case of a sick eight-year-old girl whose mother can't afford her much-needed asthma medication, leading to a legitimate question for the show's writers: Is this depiction realistic, or simply idealistic? Although the latter is probably the correct answer, the show's intent is clearly to turn the question away from itself and toward real-life health-care professionals. Why does the sight of a doctor going above and beyond the call of duty meet with audience incredulity? Is this attitude itself based on reality, or is it an unwarranted perception held by the vast majority of the American population? These are the kinds of tough questions ER refuses to shy away from. Much to the writers' credit, they also refuse to offer easy answers to them. The truth is that most doctors really would do anything within their power to help a patient — witness Mark's Herculean efforts to find a heart to transplant into a desperately ill patient — but Doug pushes the professional envelope until he enters the personal sphere. Few doctors may do this, but it's some comfort to think that perhaps few doctors possess the recklessness that would prompt them to.

"Chicago Heat"

Season 1, Episode 6

ORIGINAL AIR DATE: October 20, 1994
WRITTEN BY: John Wells (teleplay) and Neal Baer (story)
DIRECTED BY: Elodie Keene
GRADE: A-

Anyone familiar with the recent stories of weather-related distress in Chicago but unable to understand how anything less apocalyptic than a hurricane, tornado, or flood could possibly endanger people's lives should find this episode an eye-opener. When a sudden heat wave grips the city, the ER is filled with people suffering its effects, people who, presumably, don't have the wherewithal to afford air-conditioning or even properly ventilated housing. This is simply one of the realities of living in a city like Chicago, and ER seizes upon its setting here to present a gritty, powerful depiction of big-city survival. Although the story of Doug's treatment of a little girl who has suffered an accidental cocaine overdose may seem unrelated to the heat wave, the tacit connection between the two is that the same inner-city social problems that prevent people from coping with the heat are the very ones which cause such horrific overdoses.

This class-oriented episode drives its point home through the day-long presence of Mark's daughter, Rachel, in the ER. Although she's there, ostensibly, to allow Mark the chance to explain their ever-more-confusing family life to her, she is also meant to remind us how easily she might be that overdosed little girl were their circumstances reversed. And while some will find it hypocritical for a show owned by mega-corporations General Electric (of which NBC is a subsidiary) and Warner Bros. to preach social gospel, this effect is mitigated somewhat by the reminder, in the form of the sudden appearances of Susan's troubled sister, Chloe, that it's not only the lower classes who suffer such problems.

Each of these apparently separate story threads stands on its own, but they are nonetheless attached to one another thematically in this complex and thought-provoking episode.

"Another Perfect Day"

Season 1, Episode 7

ORIGINAL AIR DATE: November 3, 1994
WRITTEN BY: Lydia Woodward (teleplay) and Lance Gentile (story)
DIRECTED BY: Vern Gillum
GRADE: B

Chloe, who has managed in a little less than two full episodes to become one of the least appealing characters on network television, storms back into Susan's life just in time to ruin her already hectic birthday. Sherry Stringfield plays her complicated character to perfection, although even she must find it difficult to shift gears between playing take-charge Dr. Lewis one moment and ambivalent sister Susie the next. Of course, similar demands are placed on Anthony Edwards, because Mark is also caught in the tension of trying to perform up to snuff at work while his family life is going to hell in a handbasket. He spends yet another lonely night without Jenn, and the question for him and Susan isn't *if* cracks will begin to show in his professional facade, but *when*.

ER makes one wonder how anyone not hermetically sealed into a container after work, and thus kept free from personal distraction, can possibly survive the stress of emergency medicine. God knows Carol hasn't found a way to sort through her messily overlapping personal and professional lives yet, and if her sudden lip lock with Doug is any indication, her character is going to be a flash point for weeks to come. Maybe it's only by leaving their emotions at the door and plunging headlong into this line of work with a single-minded devotion to the technical side of the profession that these doctors are able to maintain their sanity. It certainly seems to work for Benton, whose most personal story line to date involves his interview this week for the prestigious Stargill Fellowship and his doubts as to whether to believe Dr. David Morgenstern's positive appraisal of him or Nurse Haleh Adams's more earthy criticism. The fact that he even takes the time to be bothered by Haleh's opinion does suggest there's more to Benton than meets the eye; we simply haven't seen much of it yet. Here's hoping that the writers pay more attention to character in the coming weeks. This week's other stories are painful reminders that La Salle hasn't been given the same dramatic opportunities as his fellow cast members. He deserves his turn at bat.

"9½ Hours"

Season 1, Episode 8

ORIGINAL AIR DATE: November 10, 1994
WRITTEN BY: Robert Nathan
DIRECTED BY: James Hayman
GRADE: C-

This is an oddly unsatisfying episode of ER. It's not so much that nothing happens as that what does happen doesn't seem likely to lead anywhere in particular. Case in point: Carter's crush on Susan, who's not getting along with Div too well these days. Any viewer who stops and thinks about it for a moment realizes this can't possibly be going anywhere. First, Susan is still levelheaded enough to know that her life could only be made worse by hooking up with a medical student. Even if doing such a thing wouldn't violate the hospital's code of conduct, it would make working in the ER impossible — how seriously, for instance, would Benton take her if he learned that she was involved with Carter? Second, even someone as sweetly moronic as Carter knows he'd be stepping over the line by pursuing his feelings. This is a case of puppy love, pure and simple. It would be much more fruitful to write Carter into a legitimate relationship with someone his own age — preferably someone from outside the hospital — and explore the personal life of a medical student a little more closely. We're surely seeing plenty of Mark's, who spends the day at home to be with his wife. Why not spread it around a little more?

The story that works best this week is that of a suicidal rape victim whom Carol comforts. The writers address a disturbing situation with grace and sensitivity, and Julianna Margulies does a wonderful job of channeling her own character's post-suicide-attempt angst into compassion in her scenes with the young woman. While it's true that including more meaty stories in the episode might have distracted from the gravity of Carol's thread, adopting this mind-set really does sell Margulies's talents short and underestimates the ability of the show's viewers to extract an episode's essence from among a variety of well-written plots. Some bets were hedged in this episode, and, as a result, there's not nearly as big a payoff as there might have been.

"ER Confidential"

Season 1, Episode 9

ORIGINAL AIR DATE: November 17, 1994
WRITTEN BY: Paul Manning
DIRECTED BY: Daniel Sackheim
GRADE: A-

If last week's episode was disappointing from the standpoint of its writing, this week's succeeds on those very grounds. The writers take some chances here, involving Cvetic, Carter, and Carol in three separate ethical situations that leave the viewer with plenty to chew over. Cvetic, who's been battling depression recently, is enough of a psychiatrist to know that his growing hostility toward his patients is healthy neither for them nor for him, but it's not clear that he'll be willing to step away long enough to help himself, let alone accept that help from someone else. Carter suffers similar self-doubts when he has to confront his own behavior while reluctantly treating a transvestite. And Carol is faced with the most daunting dilemma of all when the victim of a car accident admits to her that he's lied to the police by blaming the crash on his dead friend.

The first of these stories raises the issue of how the psychological well-being of health-care professionals can impact patients. And if a psych consult can fall victim to the pernicious energies of clinical depression in this way, then what might the implications be for an ER staffer suffering from the same problem? This might be worth thinking about by anyone who has ever complained about gruff treatment from a doctor who is presumed to have a perfect life.

Carter's story takes a bigger chance because it depends on the openmindedness of the American public for its success. Unfortunately, there is that segment of the population that won't see anything wrong with Carter's attitude. The writers do maximize the chances of alerting viewers to their own biases by choosing to employ Carter here; his boy-next-door image strikes a chord with the audience, so he may be more persuasive in making a statement against prejudice than a character like Benton might have been.

It's Carol's story, however, that's the most compelling of the three because it raises the loaded issue of confidentiality in the professional sphere and parlays it into an insight into her relationship with Tag. After hearing the confession, she tells Tag she has slept with Doug once since she and Tag have been together. This leaves both of them in a tenuous situation, although Tag is so blinded by love that he's unlikely to break it off with her. What remains to be seen, if her revelation was, as it seems, intended as a hint to Tag, is whether Carol and the writers will have enough courage and compassion to end the relationship before it's too late.

"Blizzard"

Season 1, Episode 10

ORIGINAL AIR DATE: December 8, 1994
WRITTEN BY: Lance Gentile (teleplay) and Neal Baer and Paul Manning (story)
DIRECTED BY: Mimi Leder
GRADE: A

The initial mood in this slightly schizophrenic episode is set by Jerry, who sings merrily as he plows through the heavy snowfall in his oversized boots and parka on the way to work. His lighthearted mood carries over to Cook County, where nothing much is going on because of the blizzard. The staff occupies itself by playing games in the halls, and Mark and Susan get into the swing of things by placing a plaster cast on Carter's leg while he sleeps. It's amusing to see everyone letting down his or her professional guard for a while, but luckily the entire episode isn't devoted to childish antics. As we find out soon enough, the first third of the show is intended merely to lull the doctors — and ER's audience, no doubt — into a false sense of security, because before long the ER is inundated with patients following a 32-car pileup. The controlled chaos of the remainder of the episode is tightly directed and interestingly plotted. Instead of just hitting its viewers with a barrage of medical practice, the writers throw in some surprises: Carol announces her engagement to Tag, Doug inadvertently causes a patient's death by mislabeling him, and Bob performs a lifesaving surgical procedure on a man who would otherwise have been a goner. There's almost too much to keep track of here, but the writers go ahead and choose this as the best moment also to introduce a new character, Dr. Angela Hicks. Some skillful editing strings all the action together, and the only weakness of the episode is its hokey segue from levity to gravity, during which, in overly dramatic silence, preparations are made to accept the multitude of accident victims who are on their way to the hospital. But this is only a minor flaw in an otherwise fine episode.

"The Gift"

Season 1, Episode 11

ORIGINAL AIR DATE: December 15, 1994
WRITTEN BY: Neal Baer
DIRECTED BY: Felix Enriquez Alcalá
GRADE: B

It's Christmas in the ER, and the question of the season is this: What do you take from the person who has everything? Well, if you're Benton, you take his liver, his kidney, his heart, et cetera. At least that's what it looks like when he makes like Dr. Santa Claus by planning to dole out a dying man's organs to transplant-patients-in-waiting as if the organs were so many stocking stuffers. The only problem is that he hasn't yet had the organ release forms signed, which places him and the patients depending on him in limbo while they wait for due process to be conducted. That Benton, such a stickler for procedural detail, would set this confusion in motion by bending the rules is quite out of character for him, and indicates either that his character is loosening his clinical grip in favor of some compassion or that he's just been struck by a bout of yuletide cheer. If it's the former, we can expect some benefits in the character-development department to be reaped before long. If it's the latter, then it's just the latest in a long series of Christmas-story cop-outs that turn up in programs of all stripes at this time of year, but to which ER's writers will, with any luck, not lower themselves.

Meanwhile, the torch singer, "Madame X," makes a return appearance that puts Carter in the mood for love. He tries to plant a wet one on Susan, who deflects it with grace, good humor, and a hilarious look on her face. Maybe she could have used the affection, given the fact that Div disappears from her life and the show without a trace, but it was evident from the moment this idea was raised that she and Carter weren't going to be an item. Now Noah Wyle can devote his talents to playing something other than the lovesick young med student.

A solid, if unspectacular, episode that avoids the maudlin pitfalls of most Christmas shows.

"Happy New Year"

Season 1, Episode 12

ORIGINAL AIR DATE: January 5, 1995
WRITTEN BY: Lydia Woodward
DIRECTED BY: Charles Haid
GRADE: B+

Peter's personal life is finally given some attention after his sister approaches him about putting their mother in a nursing home. He, of course, resists the idea simply because it just doesn't seem right to him, and pledges to find a viable alternative. Although the idea is never stated outright, his insistence that his mother not enter a home raises the possibility that his obstinate and arrogant pursuit of his career goals may be part of a larger desire to please his mother. It's

best that this fact, if it is one, be left unsaid for now so that Benton
doesn't get caught in an ill-advised story line that would impede
genuine character development. So far, so good. And as Benton's
character develops, so does Carter's. Now that he's been divested of
his crush on Susan, he's addressing the more appropriate issue of his
career, demanding that Benton give him an opportunity to do more
than "scut work." For her part, Susan, having rid herself of Div and
Carter, also escapes Chloe's influence when her sister runs off to
Texas with her new boyfriend. But she's barely had time to enjoy her
freedom from these annoyances before she runs up against Dr. Jack
Kaysen, an arrogant little weasel of a cardiologist whose disagree-
ment with one of Susan's diagnoses leads to a patient's death. What's
worse, he then blames *her* for the misdiagnosis. Susan's character
hasn't been given a break for a while now, and she doesn't seem likely
to be given one anytime soon. Kaysen proves an interesting addition
to the show. He's so teeth-grindingly detestable that he's almost
likable in a way; he's a character we're going to love hating, and
should provide the opportunity for Susan to score some character
points further down the road.

"Luck of the Draw"

Season 1, Episode 13

ORIGINAL AIR DATE: January 12, 1995
WRITTEN BY: Paul Manning
DIRECTED BY: Rod Holcomb
GRADE: C+

As if putting up with the eminently irritating Dr. Kaysen weren't
enough, Susan now questions her station in the hospital, and Mark's
loyalty to her, after Morgenstern gives her a not-so-gentle hint that
he's displeased with her lack of confidence in the ER. The reprimand
hurts, but not as much as her realization that it's based on Mark's
report on her performance, which raises the vexing question of how
much loyalty a doctor should expect from a friend and supervisor
when lives are at stake. Oddly enough, the very plot twist that drives
a wedge between Susan and Mark introduces a spark into their
relationship that alters their chemistry for the better, even while
they're at each other's throat. They both still have personal problems
to work out, of course, and Mark is still a married man, if not happily
so, but there's more going on here than a dispute between friends.
Given that current ER romance is nothing to brag about — Carol's
announcements of her wedding plans with Tag are still ringing
hollow — it may be that Susan and Mark will show an interest in one
another after they settle their differences. But whether Susan or Mark

would be believable adulterers is another matter altogether, so those hoping for a quick consummation shouldn't hold their breath.

The only other noteworthy event in this episode is Carter's introduction of a new medical student, Deb Chen, to the routines in the ER, which begs the question of why he's still around himself. Most med-student rotations last eight to 12 weeks at most, but he's been around for 16 already and shows no signs of heading toward the exit. But before too many viewers complain about this lapse in the show's reality, they should keep in mind how upset they'd be if Carter had just — poof! — been written out of the show at the end of eight weeks. Something big is bound to happen by the time sweeps week arrives, but for now it seems that a little too much is being held in reserve. The result is an episode that manages to be only sparsely dramatic.

"Long Day's Journey"

Season 1, Episode 14

ORIGINAL AIR DATE: January 19, 1995
WRITTEN BY: Robert Nathan
DIRECTED BY: Anita Addison
GRADE: A

Whew, long day is right! This is just the kind of tense episode that ER's writers can come up with when they need to kick-start the heart of the series, and they apply the paddles perfectly in this tightly written, breathlessly directed episode. The only difficulty here is in trying to decide who wins the award for having the longest day in this chock-full-o'-conflict episode. Let's see. There's Susan, who takes up smoking in anticipation of being upbraided for challenging Kaysen, but the doctors side with her and don't seem too thrilled with Kaysen's attitude toward residents. So maybe it's Kaysen who's had the longest day. As if losing this battle isn't bad enough, he's admitted later in the day with heart problems and becomes — you guessed it — Susan's patient. Trouble is, it's hard to imagine mustering much audience sympathy for this self-righteous schmuck. But speaking of self-righteous, there's always Benton, who solves the problem of caring for his mother by hiring Jeanie Boulet, only to be badgered by his sister for his decision. Or how about Carter, who fears that Deb Chen, with her photographic memory, may be more competent than him in the ER? Carol and Tag are clearly out of the running, since their biggest worry is that he has left their edible massage oil under the admissions desk.

No, none of these will do. The ER's Eugene O'Neill Award for the Longest Day's Journey into Night goes to Dr. Douglas Ross. On top of clashing with Tag and standing stranded with the baby of a woman who has committed suicide, he works on the case of a boy being abused by his kid sister, tells a boy with a broken leg that he actually has cancer, and treats a young man with cystic fibrosis who's worsened his condition by pulling a girl from a burning building. As if all this isn't enough, he is turned down by a woman who tells him that a friend of hers has already been burned by the love doctor himself. It may suck to be Doug Ross, but it's great to be George Clooney when you've got scripts like this to work with.

"Feb. 5, '95"

Season 1, Episode 15

ORIGINAL AIR DATE: February 2, 1995
WRITTEN BY: John Wells
DIRECTED BY: James Hayman
GRADE: B+

A collective "Did I just see what I thought I saw?" no doubt escaped the lips of ER's viewership after this episode. A woman with breast cancer is admitted in incredible agony and asks that she be allowed to die in dignity. But the staff can't administer any more morphine for fear of triggering respiratory failure. Flash ahead to Mark, standing alone over the recently deceased woman, and, given his avoidance of Susan's questions, it's clear that he's put her out of her misery by giving her the morphine. By all accounts, this sort of thing happens in hospitals all the time, but is never spoken about. Susan's tacit acceptance of what has obviously happened thus hits the daily double: it's professionally accurate and dramatically powerful. Now if Mark could only act as decisively in smoothing things over with his wife regarding Morgenstern's offer of the attending-physician position for next year.

With the possible exception of the fallout from Benton's disrespect for nurses and his run-in with Jeanie, who informs him that his mother needs more care than he's ever acknowledged, the remainder of this episode is pretty lightweight stuff. Deb Chen, with her elaborate handouts and fabulous computer simulation, shows Carter up in a trauma presentation. A snakebite victim's attacker escapes and slithers for cover through the ER. The madcap adventures continue when Carol leads a covert unit of ER staffers into Cardiology to retrieve some hijacked crash carts. *The Great Escape* it ain't, but this episode is a strange balance of gravity and levity that somehow works in spite of the distractions it presents itself.

"Make of Two Hearts"

Season 1, Episode 16

ORIGINAL AIR DATE: February 9, 1995
WRITTEN BY: Lydia Woodward
DIRECTED BY: Mimi Leder
GRADE: B

Carol's character is front and center for the first time in a long time, and she steals the show by befriending a Russian girl, Tatiana, who is abandoned in the ER by her adoptive mother. It turns out the little girl has AIDS and the mother can't bear getting close to her only to watch her die, so Carol steps in to ease the girl's loneliness. Even though Carol's maternal instincts seem, like her quite serviceable Russian, to come out of nowhere, this story works because both characters manage to hit their marks on precisely the same emotional level. Because neither character gets written into a corner here — Carol manages not to play the doting caregiver, and Tatiana is more than just a cute but pathetic kid — they connect in this episode as two fundamentally lonely people who really need one another at this moment. Unfortunately, much of the rest of the episode shows none of the balance that we find in this plot. The ongoing story of Susan and Kaysen, for instance, takes a turn for the worse when he is released after his heart trouble and promptly gives her a bouquet of flowers and a sugary "Happy Valentine's Day." Things get even weirder when he expresses an interest in her career, offers to be her mentor, and, unbelievably, asks her out to dinner. As irritating as Kaysen's character has been in the past, his sudden smarminess is even harder to take than his former priggishness. This story is going nowhere, and should probably not even have come as far as it has. Granted, it's the show's Valentine's Day episode, but that's hardly license for the writers to allow such a lapse in script quality just to engineer a peace between Mark and Susan, who go ice-skating so she can avoid Kaysen's dinner invitation.

"The Birthday Party"

Season 1, Episode 17

ORIGINAL AIR DATE: February 16, 1995
WRITTEN BY: John Wells
DIRECTED BY: Elodie Keene
GRADE: D

It didn't take long to see where the thread with Carol and Tatiana was leading. The little girl is taken to an AIDS hospice for children, and Carol contemplates adopting her to rescue her from the loneliness she'll suffer there. Needless to say, this doesn't sit too well with Tag, and the couple argue about their wedding yet again. Ho hum. Another reminder, of course, that Tag is not the man for Carol. She needs someone who understands the needs of sick children. And who would that be? Well, Doug, of course. After all, while Tag is busy trying to keep his distance from the Tatiana issue, Doug is attending to one young boy who's been shot by another and a child suffering from malnutrition. Lest we miss the point that Doug is a wonderful defender of children, he also takes time to deck a man who's been abusing his daughter. It's all just too conveniently connected here, and the writers only prevent themselves from going way too far by showing us the repercussions of Doug's actions, which include a session with a psychologist and a trip to face the review board. The writers have included all the elements of successful drama here, but something is lost in the assembly.

The rest of the episode is concerned with birthday parties gone awry — for Mark's daughter, Benton's mother, and, because of Carter's well-intentioned mistake, Benton himself. In each case, the story falls nearly as flat as the birthday party itself because all it does is remind us too glibly of something we already know: Mark is a well-intentioned but busy father, Benton can't escape the clutches of his career, and Carter is a bit of a goof. As with the Tatiana-Carol-Tag-Doug stories, the problem here is that the writers labor to construct overly simplistic connections between the stories and are left with little of substance to show for their efforts.

"Sleepless in Chicago"

Season 1, Episode 18

ORIGINAL AIR DATE: February 23, 1995
WRITTEN BY: Paul Manning
DIRECTED BY: Christopher Chulack
GRADE: A

The week's episode provides just what the script doctor ordered to get the show out of its winter doldrums: a big dose of depression with a spoonful of humor to help wash it down. Some real drama is finally injected into Benton's relationship with his mother when, after he sleeps through the alarm and doesn't give her her medication, she starts downstairs and takes a nasty tumble. Now, after weeks of playing the guilty son while arranging little more than an administrative solution to his mother's condition, he has to face the brute physicality of his responsibilities, which should open up new possibilities for his character. The writers do a fine job of shifting the episode's weight from this story to that of Carol and Tatiana, in which Julianna Margulies is given the chance to reach down and play her character with raw emotion. Carol learns that her adoption of Tatiana is being denied because of her suicide attempt and runs blindly, in a state of near hysteria, to Doug for comfort. Thankfully, for the sake of Carol's character and the show's integrity, Doug does an admirable job of preventing her from kissing him in a moment of misdirected emotion. This simple act accomplishes a lot. Carol is allowed to show the depth of her pain, Doug is allowed to show that he's not simply a cad, and the viewer is allowed to wonder, just for a moment, whether these two characters will ever end up together again. All in all, this is just a superbly written and acted story.

And although ER's attempts at comic relief sometimes backfire, this week's, in which Mark takes advice from a doctor from the Sloan School of Management at MIT, only to find that he's actually a patient from the psych ward, is executed perfectly. The humor of the situation is seamlessly turned over for dramatic purposes, however, when Jenn tells Mark that she's leaving him. Everything just seems to click in this episode.

"Love's Labor Lost"

Season 1, Episode 19

ORIGINAL AIR DATE: March 7, 1995
WRITTEN BY: Lance Gentile
DIRECTED BY: Mimi Leder
GRADE: A+

Those viewers who've always thought the airing of an episode of ER with a simple plot/subplot structure would be the last of the seven signs before the apocalypse are probably still listening for the trumpet of Armageddon to sound. They might as well stop listening, because the writers' decision to put all the show's eggs in one basket is an unqualified success. Anthony Edwards musters all the physical and emotional energy he possesses to portray Mark facing the toughest case of his career: a pregnant woman who, having recently been released after being diagnosed with a bladder infection, collapses and is brought back to the ER. Her obstetrician isn't around, so Mark decides to induce labor and is forced to perform a very ugly C-section. Baby and mother are left in rough shape, and so is Mark after the OB finally shows up to harangue him for his messy work. The mother dies, the baby lives, and Mark breaks down on his way home after a shift that must have been nearly as exhausting for Edwards to play as it would be for a doctor to experience.

The subplot, in which Benton's mother is wheeled in with her broken hip while he's busy feeling sorry for himself, is nearly an afterthought in one of the bloodiest and most fast-paced episodes to date. Perhaps only the series premiere can come close to matching this one for action and drama. Definitely not the feel-good episode of the year, but certainly one of the best.

"Full Moon, Saturday Night"

Season 1, Episode 20

ORIGINAL AIR DATE: March 30, 1995
WRITTEN BY: Neal Baer
DIRECTED BY: Donna Deitch
GRADE: C

It was bound to be difficult to live up to last week's excellent episode, but this one seems hardly to try. Maybe this week's sheer goofiness is supposed to lighten the load after "Love's Labor Lost," but it just drops it. The usual complement of lunatics shows up in the ER with full-moon fever, chief among them a werewolf, leading one to wonder why the writers would fritter away the dramatic momentum they'd established to air out this marginally comedic material. Even Mark's struggle to deal with his guilt over the botched delivery is tainted by the episode's silliness when he runs up against his new spandex-clad biker boss, Dr. William Swift. And then there's Deb Chen, whose ultra-perky competitiveness has lost whatever endearing qualities it once possessed and who is now merely as annoying for ER's viewers as she's been for Carter. She does get a mild come-uppance when, in her zest to prove herself a more prolific stitcher than Carter, she misses the opportunity to massage a gunshot victim's heart, but who really cares anymore?

If this episode is to be remembered for anything other than Diane's ethereal afterglow following a night with Doug, it will be for the fact that Benton, for the first time in videocassette-recorded history, admits that he's wrong about something. After visiting his mother and finding her in restraints, he confronts Jeanie, who tells him she ordered the restraints because Mother Benton kept trying to climb out of bed. Benton removes the restraints, leading his mother to take yet another tumble and him to apologize to Jeanie and ask her advice on a nursing home. As poignant as this story is, it gets lost in all the pointless machinations of the rest of the show. It's still better than almost anything else on television, but episodes like this lead one to wonder just how many very good shows a network television program can be expected to air in a single season.

"House of Cards"

Season 1, Episode 21

ORIGINAL AIR DATE: April 6, 1995
WRITTEN BY: Tracey Stern
DIRECTED BY: Fred Garber
GRADE: B

The writers seem to have realized what the viewers have been suspecting for a little while now: Deb Chen has outlived her usefulness in her present form, and she either has to have her character spruced up or be written out of the show altogether. It looks as though the latter will happen after she screws up a solo attempt at a central line on a junkie — a procedure she's not allowed to perform — and has to be bailed out by Carter and Benton. She tells Carter she's going to quit because she's come to the conclusion that she's just not caregiver material. With any luck, she'll take the time to pursue her true calling: tenure as a five-time *Jeopardy!* champion.

Just for the sake of balance — or maybe it's payroll — Deb's imminent departure is signalled by an incoming character, Susan's sister, Chloe, who looks like a hard case and is bound only to make Susan's life harder than it already is. Something profound is destined to happen between them, but it's too early to tell what it is. Meanwhile, if Chloe is in and Deb is out, Mark seems to be neither right now. He's butting heads with Swift, who openly contradicts Mark's diagnosis in front of a patient and asks him to discuss the "Love's Labor Lost" fiasco at a case conference, and misfires in an attempt to reconcile with Jenn.

All of this, in as ironic a twist as ER has taken to date, leaves Doug looking like a father figure as he buys Diane's son a new bike and even has a very parental-sounding squabble with her about spoiling little Jake. Is Doug really settling down, or are the writers just setting him up for a fall? Since we're heading into the home stretch of the first season, the latter scenario seems more likely, but it would be interesting to see how long the writers would be willing to sustain this character in a devoted relationship, especially given their willingness to play on the spark between him and Carol whenever necessary for audience titillation.

"Men Plan, God Laughs"

Season 1, Episode 22

ORIGINAL AIR DATE: April 27, 1995
WRITTEN BY: Robert Nathan
DIRECTED BY: Christopher Chulack

Mark's marriage continues to run on empty, and he's reminded of his troubles by the convenient parade of dysfunctional families that pass through the ER, including the mother of a murderer who hopes that her son will die of the gunshot wounds he's suffered. This gritty story is made even more disturbing by the mother's insistence that her son is "el diablo." Her words add an eerie edge to the episode, even if the story itself is a rather obvious reminder to us that the other wayward son of the show, Benton, isn't the most evil child in the world. In fact, Benton seems to be thawing out after his rough times with his mother. He actually talks to a young patient in a gentle tone, and later tracks down another doctor in the rain to arrange the transfer of a young boy with an aneurysm. It's well worth asking what's brought all this on, and the answer seems to be — if his dinner with Jeanie is any indication — that he's a young doctor in love. Whether he'll be willing to continue his nice-guy routine while he plays second fiddle to Jeanie's husband remains to be seen, but giving Benton a love interest, no matter how ill-fated, will offer his character some much-needed life outside the hospital. But as potentially damaging as this relationship may be, it's Doug's sudden seriousness about Diane that's most worrisome because it may be nothing more than a misdirected reaction to Carol's impending wedding. Viewers should savor this committed side of Doug's character while they can, because chances are it won't be around for long, especially if he continues to be tempted by Linda Farrell and the writers want to play it smart and milk the possibility of a relationship between him and Carol for all it's worth.

"Love among the Ruins"

Season 1, Episode 23

ORIGINAL AIR DATE: May 4, 1995
WRITTEN BY: Paul Manning
DIRECTED BY: Fred Garber
GRADE: C-

Get out your scorecards, because keeping track of ER's relationships is only going to get more confusing. First there's Mark. He's still not getting along with Swift, but he's been living with Jenn in Milwaukee for the past week, and they're at least sharing the same bed again. Things may finally be looking up for Mark "It Ain't Easy Being" Greene on the home front. While Mark and Jenn work on keeping their marriage together, Carol and Tag are still trying to get theirs off the ground. He seems much more sincere than she does and is justifiably miffed when she invites Diane Leeds to the wedding. He doesn't want Doug there, and who can blame him? Benton, meanwhile, looks like he's about to make his move on Jeanie despite his brother's warning that married women are nothing but trouble. And Susan tells Chloe to pack up her things and move out after she hits her up for money and skips a pre-natal appointment. As if things weren't leaning toward the soap operatic already, we also find out that Carter — or at least his father — is independently wealthy. It seems that dear old Dad Carter just happens to be worth, oh, $200 million, thus answering one of the program's niggling questions: How can Carter afford to be such a sharp dresser on an intern's budget? It's all a bit much to keep track of, but tune in next week for the continuation of these and other stories on another exciting episode of *General Hospital Prime Time*.

"Motherhood"

Season 1, Episode 24

ORIGINAL AIR DATE: May 11, 1995
WRITTEN BY: Lydia Woodward
DIRECTED BY: Quentin Tarantino
GRADE: A-

Those viewers secretly wishing that Harvey Keitel or Samuel L. Jackson might turn up in the Tarantino-directed episode will hopefully not be too disappointed that, apart from some gory touches — the gang member who shows up missing an ear, à la *Reservoir Dogs*, for instance — this episode does not stray from established ER practice. Which is good, considering that the major networks haven't been tripping over one another to air any of Tarantino's work as a movie-of-the-week.

What we do get here is a sense that things are simultaneously winding down and revving up in anticipation of next week's season finale. Carol's feet are getting colder by the second, and she and Tag continue to feud over everything from honeymoon plans to his wish for an extravagant wedding. This may open a door for Doug, whose luck finally runs out with Diane after she spots him leaving his apartment with Linda Farrell, or it might just prepare one to be slammed in his face should he now try to interfere with Carol's wedding on his own behalf. As comfortably as his character seemed to be slipping into the role of devoted companion and father, Doug's life is bound to become a lot more interesting come next week and Carol's wedding day. He can't hold a candle to Susan, though, who delivers her sister's baby on Mother's Day and will now have to look out for her sister and her newborn niece.

While it's true that much of this action has little to do with the ER — with the exception of the delivery of little Susie, it all could just as easily have been set in a law office or a grocery store — what makes this episode work is that the situations and experiences it depicts strike universal chords, and aren't limited to an audience comprised of doctors, surgeons, and nurses. Benton's desperate clinging to Jeanie as she consoles him following his mother's death is the best example of the show's refusal to confine itself to medical matters at the expense of a good story. The play's the thing on ER, and the players, in this episode particularly, do a solid job of presenting it.

"Everything Old Is New Again"

Season 1, Episode 25

ORIGINAL AIR DATE: May 18, 1995
WRITTEN BY: Lance Gentile
DIRECTED BY: Mimi Leder
GRADE: A

Much to their credit, ER's writers decided not to end the season with the frustrating series of gunshots, explosions, and other assorted cliffhangers to which lesser shows resort. After all, television viewers need closure too. Carol's relationship with Tag finally comes to an end when he goes missing from the wedding party and forces her to admit she doesn't love him the way he loves her. The question, of course, is how long it will take Doug to come a-courting. But for now the wedding celebration, if not the wedding itself, goes on as planned, becoming a fitting celebration of friends, family, and, one suspects, a first season of groundbreaking television. There's also a nice sense of closure in Carter's discovery that, with the help of Benton's very high evaluation of him, he will be offered a surgical sub-internship under Benton next year, thus bringing their relationship full circle from the beginning of the season.

All of this is not to say, of course, that some loose threads aren't left dangling to pull us back to our sofas next season. Benton is making his romantic intentions clear to Jeanie, but she's pulling away. Expect to see them together in September; that way the writers can gloss over all the messy in-between stuff and get right to the romance for the new season. News is worse for Mark, who, despite being named attending physician for next year, learns that he'll be facing a malpractice suit over the "Love's Labor Lost" case. Such a revelation would normally guarantee that Mark's character will be front and center at the beginning of next season, but he'll have some stiff competition for screen time from Susan, who comes home to dress for Carol's wedding only to find that Chloe has split and left the baby behind.

All in all a satisfying conclusion to a first-rate first season of the best show on television.

SEASON TWO

"Welcome Back, Carter"

Season 2, Episode 1

ORIGINAL AIR DATE: September 21, 1995
WRITTEN BY: John Wells
DIRECTED BY: Mimi Leder
GRADE: B+

Welcome back, indeed. It's Carter's first day as a surgical sub-intern, but he's performing more like a sweathog than a doctor. This leads, of course, to the usual round of explosions from Benton, but many of this episode's other story lines don't lead to the detonations we might expect from a season premiere. We're left wondering, for example, about the status of Mark's marriage and the legal woes that plagued him last season ("Love's Labor Lost"). Are we just supposed to forget that these things happened and start off with a clean slate? Then again, now that he's been named attending physician, he has other fish to fry. The challenge for his character, and thus for the writers, will be to ride out the transition from colleague to superior without doing too much damage to the precarious personality balance in the ER. And if Doug's reaction to Mark's decision to appoint the much-feared Kerry Weaver as new chief resident is any indication, this will be a rather bumpy ride. Susan, meanwhile, continues to teeter along the emotional tightrope she's been walking ever since she started to care for little Susie, so some workplace fireworks between her and her boss seem likely.

The real masterstroke of the episode involves Benton and Jeanie, who give each other the cold shoulder all episode long. The implication is that something bad has happened between them over the summer, but just when we're bracing ourselves for an apocalyptic confrontation between them, we catch a glimpse of them in bed together before she rushes to welcome her husband home from work. It will be interesting to see how much the writers will have to tinker with Benton's authoritarian personality to accommodate him to his new and uncomfortably weakened position as the third member of a love triangle.

"Summer Run"

Season 2, Episode 2

ORIGINAL AIR DATE: September 28, 1995
WRITTEN BY: Lydia Woodward
DIRECTED BY: Eric Laneuville
GRADE: B-

All of those viewers who've persisted in claiming that ER bears a striking similarity to *St. Elsewhere* are no doubt beaming with smug satisfaction now that Eric Laneuville, who played Luther in that earlier medical drama, has directed an episode of America's most popular television program. He does a good job, too, moving the action forward at a good clip in this episode even though he has to direct — yawn — yet another of Carol's admirers through his paces. Name: Raymond Shepherd. Occupation: paramedic. Convenient plot device: Carol rides with Shepherd and his partner, Raul Melendez, on her paramedic rotation. Obligatory "aw, shucks" moment: Shepherd rides a Ferris wheel with Carol despite his fear of heights. A paramedic with a fear of heights? This seems odd, but if Laneuville, himself a real-life paramedic, can live with this unlikelihood, so can we.

What remains to be seen is whether anyone but Benton, who appreciates her cold, clinical style, can live with Kerry Weaver as new chief resident. Ironically, Weaver's chilling presence heats things up in the ER. She's an annoyance to Doug, an unwelcome competitor to Susan, and a major pain in the butt to Mark, who has to field staff complaints about her all day long while contemplating his miserable commute home to Milwaukee. But best of all, she's a welcome addition to the cast because she shakes up the comfortable personality mix in the ER just enough to cause people such as Doug and Susan to flex a little bit of the attitude that anyone driven enough to become a doctor must possess. Something has to give if Weaver's going to become a regular in the ER, and the writers have to be careful not to make this wonderfully abrasive new character into a stereotypical baddie while they let it happen.

"Do One, Teach One, Kill One"

Season 2, Episode 3

ORIGINAL AIR DATE: October 5, 1995
WRITTEN BY: Paul Manning
DIRECTED BY: Felix Enriquez Alcalá
GRADE: B+

The unflappable Kerry Weaver is the only character who's not given a good, hard shake this week, largely because she's the one doing some of the shaking. Sparks have already started to fly between her and Susan. And although it's clear that they're conducting, at least in part, a gender-oriented turf battle, the writers haven't addressed the subject openly just yet. This is tricky territory. On the one hand, same-sex competition occurs in other workplaces, so depicting its energies in the hospital setting could bear some fruit. On the other hand, ER has to be careful not to alienate its female viewership by resting Susan and Weaver's relationship on a bed of professional catfights.

More promising is Carter's awareness that he is more concerned about the repercussions his accidental piercing of a heart patient's liver might have on his own career than on the patient's life. Whether Carter will ever escape the feel-good pull of his characterization up until now remains to be seen, but allowing him the opportunity to engage in more meaningful self-examination of his own professional politics can only strengthen him as a character. Ironically, Doug Ross's *lack* of self-examination — or at least his refusal to think of his career before he acts — is a major source of his character's strength. This week he harangues the pediatrics staff upstairs for prescribing the same medication twice to a young HIV-infected boy who's now suffered an overdose, but is told by the attending pediatricians to watch his step if he values his job. Oddly enough, what makes Doug's periodic crusading easier to stomach than Carter's is his willingness to just be a jerk and have done with it. There's nothing tentative about Doug, nor about Clooney's portrayal of him, and what the character might lack in subtlety right now is made up for in the passion of his bullheaded righteousness. Now if he could only pass some of this along to Mark, who's allowed his marriage to drift into a perpetual state of intermission now that he's decided to save himself some train travel by spending work nights at Doug's apartment.

"What Life?"

Season 2, Episode 4

ORIGINAL AIR DATE: October 12, 1995
WRITTEN BY: Carol Flint
DIRECTED BY: Dean Parisot
GRADE: B+

It's about time Mark told Susan and Weaver to smarten up and stop their constant bickering. Yes, it drives Mark nuts, but it's also become an irritation for the show's viewers, who have to brace themselves against the few minutes of each episode devoted to the dramatic equivalent of fingernails dragging down a chalkboard. Yes, Susan is under a lot of stress now that she's unsure whether to adopt little Susie or give her up to a family that can devote more time to her, but how did she ever make it through the stress of medical school if she had such a complete inability to separate her professional and personal lives? Her run-ins with Weaver may have been designed to show her character's toughness and determination, but the writers may have miscalculated. These incidents don't lend any strength and self-assurance to her character at all. Instead, they leave her looking more desperately uncertain about herself than ever.

The writers do a wonderful job of alleviating some of this tension by relegating Benton to CD-changing duty in the OR after he bangs his hand in a parking-lot dispute. The humor of the scene is accentuated by La Salle's great performance here. If you listen closely enough, you can hear Benton's blood boiling as it's never boiled before. There's also some humor to Mark's paranoia when Doug brings Linda Farrell back to his place only to find that Hulda, the Finnish flight attendant, is still there. Mark flees, but Linda, Doug, and Hulda stay — which raises an issue of personal interest to countless Clooney fans. Wouldn't this be one of those occasions when a little of *NYPD Blue*'s "some scenes not suitable for all viewers" philosophy could be injected into ER? If the world didn't end when we all saw Denis Franz's naked butt filling up our television screens, then I think we'd survive a slightly more prurient look into Doug's erotic world. Just look at the smile on the guy's face, for heaven's sake.

"And Baby Makes Two"

Season 2, Episode 5

ORIGINAL AIR DATE: October 19, 1995
WRITTEN BY: Anne Kenney
DIRECTED BY: Lesli Linka Glatter
GRADE: A-

Given Doug's shoot-from-the-lip professional ethic and Mark's new position as his workplace superior, it was only a matter of time before the two of them went toe-to-toe. The catalyst for their confrontation is Doug's decision to order a second spinal tap and a series of painful procedures for the little HIV-positive boy whose care has been bungled by the hospital yet again. Predictably, tempers flare when Mark overrules Doug's decision. What's surprising is how well Mark walks the line between tough authority figure and weak-kneed friend.

Neither the writers, nor Edwards in his performance, allows either side of his personality to take over completely from the other here. It'll be interesting to see how long Mark can walk this tightrope now that his relationship with Doug is no longer strictly buddy-buddy.

The real genius of this episode, however, is the way it plays on two sides of its viewers' emotions. First we're given the story of a woman who brings in her husband after his arm has been severed in a traffic accident. This is unsettling enough as it is. But when Carol discovers that husband and wife have actually hacked the arm off themselves in order to get him into a hospital before his insurance runs out, we're meant to share her disgust with their barbarism and immorality. Later, however, the writers appeal to our own basic instincts in the story of Benton's dealings with a wife-beating policeman. Benton talks to another cop and shows him pictures of the woman's injuries. Voila! The wife beater is brought into the ER by fellow policemen. He's been beaten by his colleagues, who say blandly that he "took a fall" while chasing a suspect. Each of these stories would make for some gripping television in its own right. Together, they become part of a morality play that's more subtle than each of the in-your-face stories might suggest.

"Days Like This"

Season 2, Episode 6

ORIGINAL AIR DATE: November 2, 1995
WRITTEN BY: Lydia Woodward
DIRECTED BY: Mimi Leder
GRADE: B

Doug, Doug, Doug. What are you thinking? First you spend the night with Harper Tracy, thereby violating the hospital's code of ethics and straining your friendship with Mark even further. Then you disobey a direct order from Bernstein by admitting a boy unnecessarily. Even though Mark goes to bat for you with Bernstein — God knows why — it looks as though your goose is cooked because Bernstein has decided not to renew your funding at the end of the year, and no money means no Dougie. But wait. How likely is it that NBC is going to write the show's resident hunk out of the picture just to satisfy the narrative? Not very. Maybe this story line should have been put on the shelf for a couple of years. It might come in handy when the network has to negotiate a new contract with Clooney and finds that Batman's services don't come cheap.

In the meantime, expect more screen time for Doug Ross, which will keep America happy for at least a few weeks. Now, if only something could be done for Benton. Jeanie Boulet is back in his life, or at least in his face, now that she's a physician's assistant at County. He, of course, makes her life a living hell — until she tells him to wise up and get over their romantic past. It's nice to see Jeanie being allowed to move beyond the quiet forcefulness that has thus far marked her relationship with Peter, and it's even better to see Benton with his tail between his legs for a change. The writers are going to have to work overtime cranking out humorous subplots such as this week's betting pool on Randi's criminal past in order to lighten the mood in a suddenly nasty ER.

"Hell and High Water"

Season 2, Episode 7

ORIGINAL AIR DATE: November 9, 1995
WRITTEN BY: Neal Baer
DIRECTED BY: Christopher Chulack
GRADE: A+

It's going to be hard to outdo this one, the episode that finally lives up to its "must-see" billing. Doug lands a cushy job in private practice after learning that his funding has been cut. That night his car gets a flat in a furious rainstorm and, just as he's about to light up a joint behind the wheel (not a good career move, Doug), a boy starts pounding on his window, screaming for help. Doug runs to help the boy's brother, Ben, who is trapped in a drainage tunnel and drowning in the fast-rising water. He finally rescues Ben and commandeers a television news chopper to fly him to County. The drowning boy is, of course, a figurative representation of Doug, who, we're reminded, must save himself from his own immaturity and self-destructive impulses if he's going to survive. Most other shows wouldn't be able to make a point in this way without seeming trite, but ER pulls it off because, Doug's own problems aside, the boy's story is riveting enough on its own. Few other programs can fill the screen with action and make time stand still at the same time, but ER does it again and again.

The trial-by-water plot is so powerful that everything else in the episode seems an irritating distraction. That's a shame, especially because the efforts by Carter and Harper to save a 10-year-old hit-and-run victim and keep her parents from each other's throat could easily have been fleshed out and made the centerpiece of another episode. A little old lady's marijuana-smoking (she calls it her glaucoma medicine) and Carol's *Doom*-playing (she's kicking Mt. Sinai's butt via modem on the ER's new computer) provide some comic relief, but Superdoc Doug steals the show.

"The Secret Sharer"

Season 2, Episode 8

ORIGINAL AIR DATE: November 16, 1995
WRITTEN BY: Paul Manning
DIRECTED BY: Thomas Schlamme
GRADE: A

ER follows up the best episode of the season with another good effort — and a good decision. Although Doug is offered his job back by Morgenstern, who figures out that his sudden hero status makes for good PR for the hospital, he doesn't suddenly start acting like the employee of the month. In fact, he is sent home for the day by Mark after falsifying a child's chart and arguing over the treatment of two injured motorcyclists. By deciding not to take the easy way out and use last week's heroics as a quick fix for his character, the writers force Doug to work his way out of the mess he's thrown himself into. At the end of this episode, after he's skipped his hero's dinner in favor of shooting pool, bourbon, and his mouth off at Mark with his recitation of a sarcastic acceptance speech that sticks the fork in County's staff, Doug does show signs of straightening himself out. Mark is right. Doug's "cowboy crap" has got to stop.

Carter, on the other hand, makes like the Lone Ranger when he pays a house call to a young Hispanic boy whom he fears he may have misdiagnosed. He doesn't stand to gain much by doing this, really, since the boy's family is less than happy to see him and ER's viewership doesn't need much more convincing to believe his sugar coating hides only a syrupy-sweet center. The same may not be true, however, of Shep, the lovable lug who just can't seem to do anything right. He makes the mistake of scoffing at a teen who's tried to kill herself, saying that no one who takes pills is really serious about suicide. But Carol tells him about her own suicide attempt, and he's left without a leg to stand on because both feet are planted firmly in his mouth. Then he destroys her roof while trying to make good by fixing it, but, as usual, manages to make his screwup endearing. Oh, Shep. Will you never win? Oh, ER. Will you never stop treating Shep like his helpless puppy namesake and do something worthwhile with his character?

"Home"

Season 2, Episode 9

ORIGINAL AIR DATE: December 7, 1995
WRITTEN BY: Tracey Stern
DIRECTED BY: Donna Deitch
GRADE: B-

The fever pitch of the last few episodes finally lets up this week. Jeanie finds herself in a plot that doesn't involve Benton for a change when Josh, a young man who suffered a breakdown while studying to be an architect, comes through the ER. Her frustration with the system that allows Josh to wander from institution to institution without giving him any real help leads her to question whether the ER is really the place for her. Maybe not, but this brief look at Jeanie, free from Benton's brooding presence, indicates that ER is definitely the place for her character. If she's allowed to continue to develop her own character, instead of being forced into Benton's background, she could become a complement to Carter. Like Carter, she cares about her work, but she's also not afraid to stand up for herself — especially when Benton is in her way. For his part, Benton seems to have moved on anyway. He's too busy impressing Dr. Vucelich with his confidence in the OR to let Jeanie's concerns enter his careerist orbit.

The same can't be said of Susan, who's too preoccupied with caring for little Susie to do anything beyond her usual competent medical work. She's letting career opportunities pass her by, with no guarantee that she'll be able to retain custody of her niece. Oddly enough, it's Benton and Susan who prove complementary this week. The writers use them as examples of how easy — and potentially dangerous — it can be for doctors to lose the delicate balance between career and personal interests. But did they have to drive the point home so brutally by blindsiding Mark with the news that his wife has been having an affair with a co-worker? This seems a trifle heavy-handed, even if it does lay some groundwork for putting Mark and Susan together romantically.

"A Miracle Happens Here"

Season 2, Episode 10

ORIGINAL AIR DATE: December 14, 1995
WRITTEN BY: Carol Flint
DIRECTED BY: Mimi Leder
GRADE: C-

The miracle in this oddly unsatisfying "happy holidays" episode is the safe recovery of a young girl abducted during a carjacking. Her grandmother prays for the first time in 50 years and explains the importance of faith to Mark, whose own problems have left him with very little Christmas cheer. The writers are obviously aiming for warm and fuzzy, but they end up with worn and facile. The story of the lost child is compelling enough on its own. Is it really necessary for ER to wring every possible bit of sympathy out of its viewership by resorting to the transparent characterization of her grandmother as a concentration-camp survivor? It's all well and good to remind us that Christians don't have a monopoly on religious traditions in December, but this approach comes on too strong. And as moving as the little girl's return is, it's probably just as miraculous that Benton admits that Carter is light years ahead of him in terms of bedside manner. His decision to ask Carter to convince a patient to undergo the clamp-and-run procedure isn't exactly the same as walking on water, but it's still remarkable for Benton to admit he has a medical character flaw.

However, this new edge to Benton's character can't even come close to cutting through the episode's corn, which is played up by Carol's treatment of a jolly, white-bearded toymaker named "Mr. Calus" and her insistence on caroling for the hospital's patients whether her co-workers join her or not. It's this goofiness that makes the inclusion of a concentration-camp survivor so hard to fathom. How seriously can we be expected to take this woman's struggle for faith in an episode that slides toward the unenviable standard of yuletide giddiness set by such shows as *Beverly Hills 90210*? ER's writers should know better.

"Dead of Winter"

Season 2, Episode 11

ORIGINAL AIR DATE: January 4, 1996
WRITTEN BY: John Wells
DIRECTED BY: Whitney Ransick
GRADE: C+

'Tis no longer the season to be jolly, and the ER is crackling with conflict. Jeanie is at Benton's throat because his personal treatment of her is dismissive and his professional treatment of his patients is scarcely better. Then she goes after Carol about her student evaluation, in which Carol points out, ironically, that she needs to be more assertive. The rapid character development continues when she meets with Al and rejects his offers of reconciliation. Why the writers have chosen to let her cut a swath through the ER just now isn't apparent. Instead of adding some spice to her character, they've turned her into a red-hot chili pepper. What they haven't shown us is how, exactly, she's come to this point. As a result, her characterization is left feeling slightly empty. And because hers is the character who receives the most attention this week — despite the fact that Mark is served with divorce papers and Benton finally lands the spot on Vucelich's prestigious research team — that leaves the entire episode feeling slightly empty as well.

MOSHE SHAI / SHOOTING STAR

Part of the difficulty here is that this is, in many ways, a transition episode for the major characters. In addition to setting the stage for Mark and Benton to react to their newfound circumstances over the coming weeks, the writers also leave some room for Carol, Shep, and Carter to maneuver in future episodes. Because these other characters are placed on the back burner to simmer away by themselves for a while, Jeanie is perhaps thrust to the forefront too mechanically. She's forced to carry a heavier story load than her character is capable of at this point, and the result is an uncharacteristically flat episode. This isn't a bad episode, it's just a bland one. And ER's viewers aren't accustomed to bland TV.

"True Lies"

Season 2, Episode 12

ORIGINAL AIR DATE: January 25, 1996
WRITTEN BY: Lance Gentile
DIRECTED BY: Lesli Linka Glatter
GRADE: C

It's a sure bet that ER has hit a midseason slump when an episode's single most memorable image is Morgenstern, in a kilt and frilly shirt, digging into a steaming platter of haggis. Benton's cozying up to Vucelich continues when he attends a posh dinner party at his mentor's home and plays it meek and mild for the entire evening. But although this does afford La Salle the opportunity to subtract some volume from — and add some subtlety to — his performance, the almost childlike awe with which Benton approaches Vucelich seems too artificial, even for someone who's trying to score brownie points. The story line itself is captivating, but this week's installment takes away its sizzle without offering any steak. The same goes for Doug's current malaise, which apparently can be traced back to his poor relationship with his father. With all the melodrama surrounding this story, viewers can be forgiven if they think they've tuned in to *General Hospital* by mistake.

Carter is the only character who takes a major step forward in this episode. While Benton is off trying to place nice with the Vuceliches, Carter is learning the hard way that sometimes he has to be cruel to be kind. His reluctance to tell Ruby Rubadoux of the seriousness of his wife's condition is based largely on misguided kindness, but it's also related to his professional selfishness. Granted, he doesn't want to cause Ruby any pain, but he's more concerned with himself and how he'll deal with the awkward situation than with the elderly man's grief. We've seen this sort of doctorly denial before — in Doug's persistence in treating the HIV-positive boy in "And Baby Makes

Two," for example — but Carter's susceptibility to it, and accompanying disagreeable demeanor, are part of a more pointed moment of character development here.

"It's Not Easy Being Greene"

Season 2, Episode 13

ORIGINAL AIR DATE: February 1, 1996
WRITTEN BY: Paul Manning
DIRECTED BY: Christopher Chulack
GRADE: B

Action and character conflict have always been the cornerstones of ER, but this week we get something new: intrigue. Benton has suspicions about Vucelich's criteria for admitting patients to the clamp-and-run study and decides to investigate his records for procedural inconsistencies. On top of this, the case that raises Benton's eyebrows has had a shady history of its own already, what with Carter's decision to recommend the patient for the study after telling Harper that, despite her diagnosis, the woman is not a viable candidate. Now Carter and Benton are both in awkward positions, but their respective stories point in some promising directions. After a few weeks stuck in neutral playing Vucelich's toady, Benton's character will now have to shift gears repeatedly if he's going to fish for career advancement and evidence against his mentor at the same time. La Salle should thank his lucky stars — or the writers, at least — for being given what looks like the plum story line of the season thus far. And it may still be too early to tell if Carter's recent boorish behavior is anything more than a character blip, but the writers are nonetheless taking a risk by hanging him out to dry for a viewing public that has, to this point, liked plenty of sugar on its Carter.

Meanwhile, Mark's season-long downer continues when he learns that he may have to face the "Love's Labor Lost" litigation without the hospital's support and that his wife is suing for full custody of Rachel on the ground that he's "a distant and absent father." Thankfully, Susan, who's been nearly invisible in recent weeks, wins one for the good guys when she finally gives Weaver a piece of her mind. But for those viewers who were getting to like Weaver despite — or perhaps because of — her crabbiness, her suggestion that she's been annoying Susan on purpose to see how well she'd stand up to it is a bit much. Crabbiness is one thing; deliberate psychological torture is quite another. The real crime here is that the writers were apparently unable to find any way of working Susan back into the mix other than to exploit the flattest feature of Weaver's character. Both characters, and all of ER's viewers, deserve something more complex and significant than this weak brushback pitch.

"The Right Thing"

Season 2, Episode 14

ORIGINAL AIR DATE: February 8, 1996
WRITTEN BY: Lydia Woodward
DIRECTED BY: Richard Thorpe
GRADE: B+

What are the writers doing with Carter? He's been the anti-Benton all along, but now he's doing a pretty mean Benton impersonation every chance he gets. In past weeks he's mistreated Mr. and Mrs. Rubadoux and betrayed Harper, and now he's adopted a generally nasty attitude in the ER, berating two street alcoholics (one of whom has AIDS) who get drunk in an examining room and issuing a feeling-sorry-for-himself apology to Ruby Rubadoux at his wife's funeral. But for all its bluster, this swerve in Carter's characterization feels more like a brief — and perhaps unnecessary — pit stop than a major change of course. His angst needs to be given some direction.

Benton, on the other hand, continues to plow straight ahead in one of the show's strongest continuing stories to date. After signing in late to surgery with Vucelich because he's been examining the clamp-and-run files all night, Benton asks him about the criteria for accepting candidates and is promptly dropped from the day's surgical rotation after receiving a thinly veiled threat. Benton asks Mark and Hicks if he should spill the beans, and both warn him to tread lightly. Benton being Benton, he confronts Vucelich again, and this time the threat is crystal clear: if Benton pursues this, he's going to be up surgery creek without a scalpel. As if the friction between him and Vucelich weren't enough, the writers thicken the plot by illustrating how two of Benton's most notable qualities — his ambition and his strong sense of principles — can function like opposite sides of a velcro strip. All we can do is sit tight and hope we don't hear the loud rip of Vucelich tearing that strip apart.

While all of this is going on, we're treated to some more titillation concerning Susan and Mark, who laughingly discuss the hypothetical implications of an even more hypothetical affair between them as they down margaritas. Yes, there's some sexual tension here, but against the backdrop of the tension between Benton and Vucelich, it just falls flat. Doug's birthday surprise — a visit from his father, Bulls tickets in hand — carries more dramatic weight, but doesn't seem to go anywhere in particular.

"Baby Shower"

Season 2, Episode 15

ORIGINAL AIR DATE: February 15, 1996
WRITTEN BY: Belinda Casas-Wells (story)
  and Carol Flint (teleplay and story)
DIRECTED BY: Barnet Kellman
GRADE: A-

Yes, it's raining babies in the ER after a sprinkler malfunction in OB/GYN forces a number of expectant mothers to be moved downstairs, and the manic delivery action ranges from the dramatic to the bizarre in one of the most eventful episodes of ER to date. Take a deep breath. Mark successfully handles the birth of twins, the second of which is a breach baby, all the while being pestered by Dr. Coburn, and he also encounters Dr. Castigliano, an attending physician at Cook County who has suspended her cancer therapy in order to have a child, and he and Doug work on a woman who sets some decibel-level records while giving birth to a 10-pounder, and Susan deals with a troubled 13-year-old girl who is having second thoughts about giving her baby up to a young couple, and she also discovers that what appear to be the perfect expectant parents are actually two gay friends who've made an arrangement so the mother and her gay lover can have a family, and Jeanie discovers an expectant mother smoking crack in a hospital bathroom, and Harper, in the evening's strangest case, treats a woman who's convinced that she's been impregnated by aliens. You may now exhale.

There's a lot going on here, obviously, and the writers do at least as good a job as the doctors of keeping the cases separate and not losing sight of the individuals involved in the frenzy of action. In non-birthing-related events, Scottie Pippen drops by for a visit, supplying some comic relief that's overly reminiscent of Kevin McHale's appearance on *Cheers* a few years ago, and Doug, who's still in search of a meaningful story line, looks for one by meeting his father for drinks and to share bittersweet memories.

"The Healers"

Season 2, Episode 16

ORIGINAL AIR DATE: February 22, 1996
WRITTEN BY: John Wells
DIRECTED BY: Mimi Leder
GRADE: A-

If you didn't see this one coming, then you've been busy watching ABC's *Prime Time Live* all season long. Just when Doug seemed to be warming up to dear old Dad, Ray stands him up for a Bulls game. Doug tracks him down and lashes out at him for his years of neglect, and realizes — surprise, surprise — that his own fear of commitment is the result of his father's absentee example. Luckily, Ray himself rescues the plot from becoming too conveniently maudlin when he reminds Doug that he's a grown man and can't lay all his troubles at his father's doorstep. This is a helpful reminder for the writers as much as Doug; if ER's viewers wanted to see people resolving their problems by passing the buck to their parents, they could just watch *Ricki Lake*. Besides, why blame your parents when you can blame your sister? That's the direction that Susan's story line seems to be taking again when, on the very day her adoption of little Susie will become official, Chloe shows up again.

But this week's real focus is . . . Shep? Yep. He and his partner, Raul, run into a burning building to rescue some children, but only Shep makes it back outside safely. Raul is nowhere to be seen, at least until he's brought into the ER, charred beyond recognition. The writers manage to convey the horror of his condition not just by showing us some grisly shots of his body, but also by allowing Carter to admit that he just can't bear to work on him. The point here is painfully clear: Suffering burns of this magnitude is surely one of the most horrific experiences a human being can have, but treating them comes a very close second. Such consistently understated attempts to show how doctors and patients can both suffer trauma from a severe injury are one of the things that ER does best. And although Shep sinks into guilt and despair for his partner's condition, the episode never sinks into melodrama. It's powerful without being preachy, and Shep finally proves himself useful for something other than mere annoyance.

"The Match Game"

Season 2, Episode 17

ORIGINAL AIR DATE: March 28, 1996
WRITTEN BY: Neal Baer
DIRECTED BY: Thomas Schlamme
GRADE: A

How can somebody who's made it through medical school be such a dimwit? It's certainly not a stretch to think that a young doctor might suffer lapses of boorish behavior, as Carter has this season. And it's hardly more surprising that such a doctor should, as he approaches a milestone in his fledgling career, disavow that behavior and promise to put his patients first, as does Carter while he awaits the results of his internship match. But how likely is it that, moments after rededicating himself to his patients and ordering a battery of tests for a young lawyer, that doctor should abandon his patient and light out for a champagne lunch in a hotel hot tub upon hearing of his match? How likely, in other words, is it that any doctor on Earth could be as thick-skulled as Carter and still be practicing medicine? When he finally returns to the hospital, he finds that Susan has taken over treatment of the lawyer, who turns out to have leukemia. Even worse, he has to admit he's been drinking on duty when Dr. Hicks asks him to scrub in for an operation, and she threatens him with expulsion. How likely is it that this doctor would still be practicing? Or that he would not be, at the very least, suspended from duty? Very likely, if your name is John Carter and you're the fresh face on the highest-rated television program in America. Let's face it: the ER could survive without Carter, but ER couldn't.

Fortunately, we're distracted from the implausibility of this story by the clash between Doug and Benton over the treatment of a young boy whose leg injury can be traced to a bone tumor that Doug missed diagnosing weeks earlier. Benton, no doubt feeling guilty for not reporting Vucelich, blows the whistle on Doug despite Mark's order to the contrary. The boy's father accosts Doug, who has arranged to pay for the boy's expensive treatment, and tells him to stay away from the child. We've seen plenty of petty animosity in the ER, but nothing like the outright hatred that Doug now holds for Benton. This must happen in hospitals all the time, but we've seen precious little of it on this show. It'll be interesting to see how the writers handle it in the weeks to come.

"A Shift in the Night"

Season 2, Episode 18

ORIGINAL AIR DATE: April 4, 1996

WRITTEN BY: Joe Sachs

DIRECTED BY: Lance Gentile

GRADE: B+

We haven't had what might be called, in ER's terms, a good old-fashioned "sew 'em up" since "Baby Shower," but this week's action should keep fans of the thrills-and-spills side of ER happy for a few weeks. Moreover, this episode doesn't just use action for action's sake. Instead, it bombards its viewers with a frenzy of activity that parallels the psychological state of Mark, the doctor at the center of it all. This latest descent into the hell that is Mark Greene's life happens when he returns to a seriously understaffed ER after having spent the day driving to Milwaukee and back. In order to move through the mountain of patients as quickly and efficiently as possible, he orders that less serious cases be treated right in the congested waiting room. And he does much of the work himself: he gives a child bourbon because the hospital is out of ethanol to counteract the anti-freeze he's ingested; discovers that a man suffering from an overdose of a drinking deterrent has been slipped AntAbuse mickeys by his teenage son; lobbies unsuccessfully against HMO policy to admit a woman showing signs of an impending stroke; and, finally, clashes with Shep when, during one of the few moments he's able to catch his breath, he witnesses a car accident while heading across the street to Magoo's for a sandwich and has to be pulled away from the wreckage so Shep can rescue a girl trapped inside. This last incident cements the essence of this episode into place. Mark isn't a superman — as Shep points out, he isn't even a paramedic — but he *is* a first-rate physician, something that's easy to lose sight of amid all the turbulence his character has been flying through of late. Once again, ER proves itself the master of the action-packed character study.

"Fire in the Belly"

Season 2, Episode 19

ORIGINAL AIR DATE: April 25, 1996
WRITTEN BY: Paul Manning
DIRECTED BY: Felix Enriquez Alcalá
GRADE: A-

Last week's episode focused almost entirely on Mark, so it's no surprise that ER writers should go out of their way to cram as many significant moments for other characters as they can into this rapid-fire hour. Susan's hope of adopting little Susie seems about to go up in flames now that Chloe appears finally to have cleaned up her act, but viewers will be forgiven for doubting whether this story will ever truly end. It's not surprising that the writers should milk Carter's relationship with Benton and the obvious sexual tension between Mark and Susan for all they can, but why drag out a story featuring Chloe's ever-unappealing character for this long? Then there's Carol and Shep, who's suddenly not looking quite so cute and goofy after only barely stopping himself from punching her when she tries to prevent him from pummelling a man who's thrown a brick at Shep's ambulance. We're reaching that point in the season when things are set up to drop or add characters for next season, so look for Shep to be shipped out very soon.

Meanwhile, Carter resorts to some very Deb Chen-like maneuvers to undermine Dale, a new surgical intern and old friend of Harper's.

The last straw is broken when Carter runs an end-around on Dale to work on an incoming trauma, and Harper calls him a weasel and tells him their relationship is over. This likely means that either her character or Carter's won't be back next season. Care to guess which one will stay? Even Benton and Jeanie get back into things this week when he owns up to a misdiagnosis he'd tried to pawn off on Jeanie. And Mark gets some action too — literally. He ends up in the sack with an infomercial director named Iris who's been videotaping trauma procedures at Cook County and hitting on him relentlessly.

Whew! Can you say "sweeps week"? I knew you could.

"Fevers of Unknown Origin"

Season 2, Episode 20

ORIGINAL AIR DATE: May 2, 1996

WRITTEN BY: Carol Flint

DIRECTED BY: Richard Thorpe

GRADE: B+

Harper is gone, having departed for a rotation in Dallas, but maybe Shep isn't on his way out after all. His mad-at-the-world routine continues when he begins to ride with his greenhorn partner, and things come to a head when he shoves and knocks unconscious a young gang member who's getting in the way of a friend's treatment. Now this may just be one more step toward the exit for the formerly cute and cuddly Shep, but if he stays the writers may have plans to plunge Carol into the sordid world of domestic abuse. The first option is probably the best bet, if only because Carol seems just as likely to clean his clock as he is to clean hers. Then again, this is a woman who not so long ago attempted suicide. Going the latter route would certainly allow the writers to give us a fuller picture of Carol's vulnerabilities, but might be more than the show's viewers could bear.

As uncomfortable as this story line is getting, things become out-and-out weird in the Benton-Vucelich plot. Benton's formal challenge of Vucelich's methods barely makes a ripple because, Benton is told by a doctor who handled the charges, Vucelich had covered his butt by including in his study a description of the very inclusion criteria Benton called into question. And there's more weirdness to come: Benton is named resident of the year after being nominated by none other than . . . Dr. Vucelich. Go figure.

Things get even weirder when Doug sleeps with Karen, his father's investment partner, and weirder still when Mark and Jenn do the same after working out a custody agreement. Add to all this Susan's precarious emotional state throughout the episode, what with her constant flashbacks of little Susie crying incessantly for her bear, Mr. B., and you've pretty much got a salable recipe for the kind of unrest necessary to set up the season finale.

If it all rings hollow somehow, we're supposed to rest easy in the faith that this flurry of seemingly directionless activity will prove worthwhile during the final episode. The writers have made only one small miscalculation: that episode is still two weeks away. So why try to lay it all out here at once?

"Take These Broken Wings"

Season 2, Episode 21

ORIGINAL AIR DATE: May 9, 1996
WRITTEN BY: Lydia Woodward
DIRECTED BY: Anthony Edwards
GRADE: C

As last week's flashbacks suggested, Susan has gone from losing her grip on little Susie to just plain losing her grip, and her personal problems are spilling over into her work. While it's true that we have to expect her to work through her grief after losing custody of little Susie, the writers have done little but assure us that, even with Chloe and Susie gone, this story has a life of its own — even when it's being told to us through Susan's visits to her therapist. With the end of the season just around the corner, the expiry date on this plot is nearly here, which will hopefully mean the return of the old Susan in time for next year's premiere. Shep's relationship with Carol — or, in other words, his character's status for next season — becomes clearer when she sides with his partner in the dispute over his shoving a teenager last week. And Doug is still at it with Karen, but discovers that his father has fled to Mexico with a big chunk of her cash. Trying to make amends, and realizing that the $25,000 his father gave him was Karen's money, he goes to his mother and gets $25,000 to undo the damage — only to find out that dear old Dad has made off with 10 times that amount. Where all this takes Doug's character is left to the imagination. Perhaps a spin-off is in the works for Clooney, in which he plays a crime-fighting pediatrician specializing in cases of paternal embezzlement.

And although you'd hardly know it from this episode, yes, this is a hospital-related program, which includes token medical stories about Mark's treatment of our friendly neighborhood ex-prostitute, Loretta, and Carter's time spent with a girl awaiting a liver transplant. In what promises to be a major story line but comes off as so much dramatic window dressing here, Jeanie's husband is admitted for flu-like symptoms and turns out to have HIV. Get ready for more on this, and brace yourselves for a rocky ride in next week's finale as the writers try to tie all this material together in a far more digestible form than they've been able to so far.

"John Carter, MD"

Season 2, Episode 22

ORIGINAL AIR DATE: May 16, 1996
WRITTEN BY: John Wells
DIRECTED BY: Christopher Chulack
GRADE: A-

What makes this a strong season finale isn't, after all is said and done, the parts of the script that have "cliff-hanger" written all over them, such as Carol's announcement, shortly after dumping Shep, that she's quitting her job because she's tired of seeing administrative policy put before patient care. Or the ominous revelation that Susan has declined the chief resident position for next year because she needs to find something else in her life other than work. Or even Jeanie's insistence that Benton have his blood tested after Al's diagnosis with HIV. The show's viewers know that neither Carol nor Susan is going anywhere, so not much in the way of suspense is bound to arise in the wake of their apparently dire pronouncements. And anyone who was awake for last week's episode had to know that Benton and Jeanie would be forced to have themselves tested following Al's bad news, so there's nothing here we didn't already know.

Oddly enough, it's this episode's one grand moment of resolution that makes it a good season finale. This day is really about Carter's final step from "Mr." to "Dr." It's his graduation day, and he's in the mood to celebrate even before Morgenstern offers him a plum spot on the red team for his surgical assignment. By the end of the day, having missed his graduation ceremonies to keep a liver-transplant patient company and having donned the spiffy new monogrammed "Dr. Carter" lab coat given to him by Benton, he decides to change his surgical assignment and remain on the blue team with Benton. The writers have put Carter through the wringer this season, dedicating more time to truly developing his character than any other, and it pays off in the finale. He's escaped the constraints of his own ego and seems to have left his attitude at the door on the day he finally becomes Dr. Carter.

SEASON THREE

"Dr. Carter, I Presume"

Season 3, Episode 1

ORIGINAL AIR DATE: September 26, 1996
WRITTEN BY: John Wells
DIRECTED BY: Christopher Chulack
GRADE: B

It's not so much that this isn't a good episode as that it somehow lacks the characteristic "oomph" that we've come to expect of an ER season premiere. Sure, the writers drop the requisite bombshell — that Jeanie has tested positive for HIV and Benton has dodged the bullet — but its impact is lessened because it's just such an obviously convenient plot device. The development of ER's characters and story lines almost always depends on dramatic tension and conflict, and by drawing last season's major dangling story thread out slowly, instead of giving it a good, hard yank, the writers provide themselves with plenty of tension-filled script material for weeks to come.

The conflict between Mark, who's now chief resident, and Weaver, the new attending physician, holds more promise because their turf war has greater potential to actually alter the broader chemistry of the ER. This becomes evident when Weaver implements the first of her grand schemes for efficiency — a patient board featuring only social security numbers and a plethora of abbreviations instead of patients' names and procedures — and Mark does away with it (to the applause of his co-workers) after it causes nothing but chaos. Carter does his bit to erode goodwill in the ER as well because, now that he's caught up in being a real doctor, he's taken to referring to members of the staff as "nurse" instead of calling them by name. He does manage to make peace with the nursing staff — after they get sweet revenge by beeping and waking him from his much-needed naps with malevolent glee — but this brief glimpse of Carter's new attitude suggests that Wyle may get to explore another side of this ever-so-sweet character.

"Let the Games Begin"

Season 3, Episode 2

ORIGINAL AIR DATE: October 3, 1996
WRITTEN BY: Lydia Woodward
DIRECTED BY: Tom Moore
GRADE: B+

Well, it's no big surprise that the rumors that Cook County will be shut down prove to be false. After all, no hospital would mean no emergency room, which would mean no ER. But the threatened closure does provide the opportunity to introduce a new character in the form of Dr. Donald Anspaugh, the new tough-as-nails chief of staff who will no doubt add a crusty edge to the show. Meanwhile, this season's campaign to tease us with hints of romance between Mark and Susan has already begun. In case it wasn't already clear that these two are perfect for one another, we're reminded of this when they run into each other while out on the latest in a series of lame blind dates. They run off for an evening of goofing around when it becomes evident that their dates have more interest in one another than Mark and Susan will ever have in either one. "Let the games begin," indeed; but keep in mind that the real game being played here is called audience titillation. Then again, it *is* an awfully fun game to play.

And speaking of games, Doug seems to have returned to his womanizing ways when he breaks a date with his young girlfriend to go out with a pretty radiologist from upstairs instead. His continuing self-destructive behavior suddenly seems a little darker, and a little less charming, given Jeanie's circumstances. Apart from the fact that she's already on the hook for her husband's medication and being ostracized in the ER by Benton, she's also coping with an illness that never seems to cross Doug's mind as he hops from one bed to another. You'd think a doctor would think twice about these things, but if Benton didn't, it isn't too much of a stretch to think that Doug wouldn't. Now if only Benton and Ross were getting along, there might be some room here for a frank man-to-man discussion on the topic of AIDS — something ER has thus far been reluctant to pursue in favor of its more heart-tugging approach.

"Don't Ask, Don't Tell"

Season 3, Episode 3

ORIGINAL AIR DATE: October 10, 1996
WRITTEN BY: Jason Cahill (teleplay and story) and Paul Manning (story)
DIRECTED BY: Perry Lang
GRADE: B+

Anspaugh's crotchety-old-doctor routine is fitting rather nicely into the ER. He's not quite as persistently cruel as Benton, who's coming down hard on the new surgical resident, Dennis Gant, but he's no Carter either. For that matter, even Carter doesn't quite seem to be Carter. He demonstrates some of the arrogance and poor judgment we saw in the season premiere by managing to get written up by Anspaugh for scheduling a fake procedure just so he can get some OR time. Anyhow, whereas Benton spends the episode trying to have Jeanie banned from treating patients with open wounds, or at least to keep her out of the trauma room when he's working there, Anspaugh works his nastiness by requiring that each doctor treat a certain number of patients per hour. Whoever scores the lowest will have the pleasure of waxing his car. The victim of this Weaver-esque system is, of course, Mark, who is burdened with a very complicated case for almost his entire shift. If Anspaugh and Weaver ever decide to form a tag team, it will most likely be Mark who'll go down for the count. And just to make his day even worse, Mark gives himself the emotional runaround when he spends so much time trying to determine whether or not to accept Susan's invitation to accompany her on her Hawaiian vacation that she eventually withdraws the offer for fear that she's somehow deeply offended him. This has the desired effect of portraying Mark as a shy, lovesick goof and, more importantly, of drawing viewers into the game of anticipation and frustration that they so love to play.

"Last Call"

Season 3, Episode 4

ORIGINAL AIR DATE: October 17, 1996
WRITTEN BY: Samantha Howard Corbin (teleplay and story)
    and Carol Flint (story)
DIRECTED BY: Rob Holcomb
GRADE: B

The writers may finally be allowing Doug to turn away from the self-destruction toward which he's been plunging at breakneck speed for three seasons, though it doesn't look that way at first. He rushes his latest (and very inebriated) conquest to Cook County when she has a seizure, but she dies despite radical attempts to save her. He has some explaining to do — to Mark and to the police — when the woman, whose name he does not even know, tests positive for cocaine. The seriousness of the day's events and, more importantly, of his lifestyle in general, seems to sink in after Carol refuses to offer him any support and he goes home to erase the messages of several women from his answering machine. Doug's ability to walk the fine line between dedicated doctor and irresponsible ladies' man has made him one of ER's most dynamic and interesting characters, but a careful shift of his priorities might be just what's necessary to keep him from becoming a soap opera-ish caricature.

We're finally seeing some exploration of the romantic implications of Jeanie's HIV to go along with the continuing drama of her professional and medical struggles. Her quietly reluctant decision not to go out with the friend of a patient hits just the right tone, registering not only her disappointment at having to pass up this opportunity, but also her realization that she may never be able to accept another. The counterpoint to this scene, provided by Benton's tantalizing encounter with his former girlfriend, Carla, drives home the pain of her situation very powerfully, although a deeper look at the romantic challenges facing people with HIV would still be very much welcome.

"Ghosts"

Season 3, Episode 5

ORIGINAL AIR DATE: October 31, 1996
WRITTEN BY: Neal Baer
DIRECTED BY: Richard Thorpe
GRADE: B+

Hallowe'en comes to the ER and brings the inevitable goofiness with it. Mark and Susan recount the story of the ghost of the fifth floor of Cook County Hospital (not exactly terrifying stuff), and we see a different side of Benton when he accompanies Abby on trick-or-treating rounds and does a handstand for some kids who demand that he do a trick for them. While this single action doesn't exactly constitute character development, it does suggest there's a kid lurking deep in the heart of Benton after all. The serious question that remains from this episode, though, is whether there's a doctor lurking deep in the heart of Carol. She and Doug spend the night touring a rough neighborhood in Anspaugh's rickety old healthmobile, but she seems much more terrified by the physics class she's taking in order to put her pre-med academic record in order.

The only real scare of this episode is the one thrown into Mark by Anspaugh, who recommends that he pick up a research project Weaver had rejected in favor of something more challenging. This confirms Mark's suspicions that Anspaugh regards him as a flunky in comparison to Weaver, but it's hardly news. What little career-oriented horror this incident provides plays second fiddle to its romantic implications, because it gives Mark the opportunity to moan about his problems to Susan, who tells him there's more to life than work. And that "more" might just include romance. Mark and Susan drink a little too much at the staff Hallowe'en party and end up on the dance floor together. But don't hold your breath expecting to see them rolling out of bed together at the beginning of next week's episode. ER hasn't strung us along all this time just to resolve the one story line that's guaranteed to keep its viewers' interest.

"Fear of Flying"

Season 3, Episode 6

ORIGINAL AIR DATE: November 7, 1996
WRITTEN BY: Lance Gentile
DIRECTED BY: Christopher Chulack
GRADE: A-

Hallelujah, somebody finally said it! Dennis Gant calls Benton a prick after Benton rejects his offer of sympathy in the case of young Megan Herlihy, a baby brought in from a car crash. This fact alone nearly qualifies tonight's episode for an A+ rating. While operating on the infant, Benton accidentally perforates her liver, leading Keaton to lay into him for his arrogance after she barely saves Megan's life. We're finally seeing Benton face an obstacle he's never encountered before: his own incompetence. And even though his attitude toward Gant suggests his arrogance will see him through his crisis of competence, it's clear that Benton is going to spend the next little while following orders instead of giving them, which will allow his character to explore some new territory.

Although Carol hasn't seemed, up to now, particularly well suited to become a doctor, her treatment of the temporary nurse who mistakenly administers potassium instead of saline to young Megan's injured brother is a reminder that she's as capable of wielding authority as any doctor in the ER, including Benton. Still, it's easier to imagine her as the ass-kicking nurse than as a doctor; she wouldn't get away with nearly as much if she became an MD. She's about as likely to become a doctor as Susan is to admit her love for Mark. Then again, Susan does stop to give Mark a peck on the cheek before she departs on her helicopter ride to retrieve the rest of the Herlihy family from their accident site. Maybe love really *is* in the air.

"No Brain, No Gain"

Season 3, Episode 7

ORIGINAL AIR DATE: November 14, 1996
WRITTEN BY: Paul Manning
DIRECTED BY: David Nutter
GRADE: B+

In each of the past two seasons, first Mark ("Love's Labor Lost") and then Doug ("The Match Game") have spent a few weeks mired in angst over serious misdiagnoses. Now it's Benton's turn to suffer some career-churning anxiety after nearly killing Megan Herlihy, and he drags Mark and Doug into his problems by attempting to make amends by persisting in his treatment of a young gunshot victim Doug has pronounced brain-dead. The plug is pulled on the boy and, mercifully, on Benton's angst before too long. Young Megan makes a miraculous recovery, and the writers avoid going down an already well-worn path. Now if they could only resist turning every conflict between Mark and Doug into a good-cop/bad-cop drama.

But this episode also has a couple of surprises, firmly establishing ER as one of the best pull-the-chair-out-from-under-you shows in recent memory. On the "oh, that's surprising" level, there's the long, energetic kiss shared by Carter and Keaton while she's treating him for the shiner administered to him by Dale Edson after their skirmish over medical ethics. On the "sweet mother in heaven, this can't be happening" level, there's Susan's sudden announcement that she's decided to transfer to Phoenix to be closer to Chloe and little Susie. This leaves Mark — and most of the American viewing public, no doubt — more than a little numb, not least because he'd finally worked up the courage, after repeated urging from Carol, to tell Susan he loves her. The romantic tension between Mark and Susan had to be resolved somehow, and for some reason frustration plays better than consummation in this instance. Maybe it's because we know that a relationship between them would alter the chemistry in the ER too much. Then again, maybe it's just that we're so darn used to being frustrated that we've grown to like it, and anything else would be a cheat. Whatever the case may be, one thing is clear: we're in for a painful television goodbye very soon.

"Union Station"

Season 3, Episode 8

ORIGINAL AIR DATE: November 21, 1996
WRITTEN BY: Carol Flint
DIRECTED BY: Tom Moore
GRADE: A

It's not quite *Casablanca*, but Susan's goodbye does turn out to be a rather classy, understated affair. She ducks out of the ER just as a parade of accident victims is wheeled in, thereby avoiding the big send-off the staff had planned for her. When the smoke clears and Mark realizes she's gone, he rushes to the train station to intercept her — but only after a reminder from Doug that if he doesn't tell her that he loves her, he'll regret it for the rest of his life. Yes, it's corny. Yes, it's cliché. But it works. Mark reaches her just as her train is pulling away and asks her to stay, telling her at last that he loves her. She can only say she's sorry as the train moves out, but then calls back that she loves him too, leaving him standing, alone and bewildered, on the platform. This scene does a remarkable job of sending Mark out on a zigzagging emotional trajectory and pulling the viewer along behind him because it resists the urge just to have her step right off the train and throw her arms around him. That would have been the easy way out, and it's to ER's credit that it recognizes the difference between easy and best.

The episode's other events pale in comparison to Susan's departure, which is saying something, considering that Lydia and the commitment-phobic Al finally get married right there in the ER. But Maggie Doyle, who's been creeping more insistently into the action since her introduction a few weeks ago, finally has some life breathed into her character when she angrily reports and promises to testify against a pregnant woman who's been brought in drunk. Not much of a replacement for Susan, but she adds a certain sexily malevolent edge to the ER.

"Ask Me No Questions, I'll Tell You No Lies"

Season 3, Episode 9

ORIGINAL AIR DATE: December 12, 1996
WRITTEN BY: Neal Baer and Lydia Woodward (story)
    and Barbara Hall (teleplay)
DIRECTED BY: Paris Barclay
GRADE: B

There was bound to be a letdown following Susan's departure, but this episode veers dangerously toward the kind of predictability that ER has generally refused to employ in the past. Just when Carol finally restores some sanity to the nursing staff by winning her battle with the administration, Mark, who's throwing himself into his work to help him forget about Susan, initiates a new color-coded duty scheme which is nearly as nightmarish as the one Weaver tried to implement earlier in the season. Mark's attempt to replace love with procedural zeal isn't simply an overly predictable character move — it's heavy-handed. Worse still, it leads to a needlessly clumsy treatment of Jeanie Boulet's continuing struggles. Mark's decision to check Jeanie's confidential personnel file after suspecting she may be HIV positive, and then to go to Anspaugh to see what can be done about her, aren't simply out of character. They're out of keeping with the show's general reluctance to force a character into a frame of mind just long enough to incite some new development in the plot. Mark's pain and Jeanie's fear of being "outed" deserved a more elegant treatment than this.

In other predictable news, Carter's whirlwind romance with Keaton is grinding to a halt because she's off to teach pediatric surgery in Pakistan. If this seems at all sudden, keep in mind that Keaton has fulfilled her dual purpose of providing Carter with a love interest and Benton with a superior he'll never be able to please. Like any piece of medical equipment that's no longer useful, she must now be phased out of the hospital.

Maybe ER is suffering from the winter blahs. Hopefully they won't last too long.

"Homeless for the Holidays"

Season 3, Episode 10

ORIGINAL AIR DATE: December 19, 1996
WRITTEN BY: Samantha Howard Corbin
DIRECTED BY: Davis Guggenheim
GRADE: B+

As its title suggests, this season's Christmas episode isn't exactly brimming with yuletide cheer. Jeanie's illness is finally out in the open after Mark and Weaver meet with Anspaugh to construct a departmental policy for HIV-positive staff. Tired of hearing the rumor mill grinding away at a frantic pace, Jeanie announces that she is the mysterious "Employee X" about whom everyone has been whispering, and she endures their stares and awkward gestures of sympathy for the rest of the day. After seeming merely to tag along in plots that have had more to do with Benton or Mark, Gloria Reuben is finally given the opportunity to grab hold of this story line and make it her own, and she does a great job. The same can be said of Clooney, who gets to put a different spin on his character when Doug actually exercises some good judgment by refusing to let Charlie, the 14-year-old prostitute he met in the healthmobile, stay with him over Christmas. Whether this marks yet another turning point in Doug's troubled history remains to be seen, but his decision does, at least, allow a more traditional Christmas story to play itself out. He takes Charlie to Carol's for the night, where she participates in the elaborate celebration of Ukrainian Christmas traditions being conducted by Carol's mother.

The warm, homey atmosphere at Carol's stands in stark contrast to Carter's celebration, which consists of curling up in bed with Keaton, some pizza, and *The Grinch Who Stole Christmas*. Carter's method of spreading Christmas cheer is ultimately empty not just because it's purely hormonal, but also because Keaton's status as a lame-duck lover suddenly makes her an uninteresting — and perhaps even unappealing — character. Had Carter chosen instead to honor his commitment to spend Christmas Eve with Gant, we might have had some insight into what makes Gant tick. Granted, this would probably have put the episode on too much of a downswing, but it would have allowed for the kind of dramatic character development that's been absent from Carter's story lines for some time now.

"Night Shift"

Season 3, Episode 11

ORIGINAL AIR DATE: January 16, 1997
WRITTEN BY: Paul Manning
DIRECTED BY: Jonathan Kaplan
GRADE: A

It's a fairly ho-hum night at Cook County, which can only mean one thing: ER is setting its viewers up for something big. The groundwork for the big event is laid out in an appropriately pedestrian fashion. Doug has another encounter with Charlie, who comes by to ask him for money to pay off a threatening pimp and is later brought in after having been raped and beaten, and Carol is still fighting the administration over budget cuts. There's a blip of intrigue when Benton, who's still aching for a second turn on the pediatric surgery rotation, walks in on Keaton and Carter sharing an affectionate moment in her office, but his arrogance won't allow him even to consider blackmailing her. He wants the position based on his merit as a surgeon, and Keaton tells him that he's just not cut out for pediatric surgery. And maybe the fact that Mark ends up in the sack with Chuny is worthy of a raised eyebrow, but not much more. He's moved on to the second stage of grief: first denial, then horniness.

But the real blood and guts of this episode is the story of Dennis Gant, which is handled superbly. After Benton rips into him right in the middle of the crowded cafeteria, Gant goes to Anspaugh to complain about Benton's persistent poor treatment of him and is disappointed when Carter won't back him up. Toward the end of the shift, the paramedics wheel in a young man whose head has been mangled beyond recognition after being hit by a train. Now the drama begins to unfold quickly and effectively. Gant, to Benton's displeasure, doesn't answer his page to come and work on the case. But the trauma team suddenly realizes that their patient's beeper is going off: it's Gant, who dies on the table despite the staff's frantic efforts to save him. The writers pull this one off magnificently, holding back the surprise until the last possible moment and leaving it entirely to the viewer to speculate whether Gant had fallen in front of the train or jumped. Although it's sad to see Gant go without having a more thorough look inside his character, his death will likely give Carter and Benton plenty of new character space to explore.

"Post Mortem"

Season 3, Episode 12

ORIGINAL AIR DATE: January 23, 1997

WRITTEN BY: Carol Flint

DIRECTED BY: Jacque Toberen

GRADE: A

Carter and Benton both feel partly responsible for Gant's death, but they deal with their guilt in completely different ways, which allows for some fine dynamic interplay between them. For his part, Carter, true to the form in which he was first presented on ER, reaches out to others in order to work through his remorse. Much to the writers' credit, Benton also keeps his character on its original course in the face of this trauma, hiding his feelings behind a beefed-up facade of arrogance instead of making the kind of emotional about-face that wouldn't really be believable from him anyway. Carter, who tells Benton that the only place his emotional isolation is going to get him is where it got Dennis Gant, seems to have inherited some of Gant's gumption, which could help take his relationship with Benton in new directions.

While all this is going on, nearly everyone else seems stuck in neutral. Doug's dealings with Charlie come to an awkward halt after she lies to Social Services about his willingness to look after her. And

Carol, who's been suspended in limbo between the administration and her staff, is hung out a little further after she accidentally kills a patient while trying frantically to cover for a staff that has called in sick in order to protest administrative cuts. Despite the apparent importance of these events — and the implications, especially, of Carol's mistake — they somehow come off as more of the same. But this minor weakness in an otherwise very good episode is made up for by the new life that's being breathed into Jeanie's character. Things take a romantic turn for her when she meets an attractive infectious-diseases expert, Greg Fischer. She's under the impression that he's gay, but he dispels this by planting a kiss on her at Magoo's, leading her to draw away for fear that her HIV has made her untouchable. This thread has some great potential, and not just because it promises to continue Jeanie's sputtering character development. It also addresses the issue of intimacy for HIV-positive people, which has not yet been done justice on television.

"Fortune's Fools"

Season 3, Episode 13

ORIGINAL AIR DATE: January 30, 1997
WRITTEN BY: Jason Cahill
DIRECTED BY: Michael Katleman
GRADE: B-

The yin-and-yang quality that runs fairly consistently through ER becomes a little too transparent this week. By now we're quite accustomed to one character's ups being offset by another's downs, but this plays itself out too mechanically here. Things finally seem to be looking up for Mark, who manages not only to impress Anspaugh with the hands-on tour of duty he provides to a group of aspiring medical students, but also to wiggle out of his awkward relationship with Chuny in time to go out on the town with an attractive patient who flirted with him mercilessly in the ER. On the other side of the seesaw is Benton, whose attitude may be putting his career in jeopardy. His latest crisis involves his playmate and former girlfriend, Carla Reese, who announces that she is pregnant with his child. He's so preoccupied with the idea of impending fatherhood that he misses a conference presentation he was to have conducted with Carter, who has had it with Benton and accepts Hicks's offer to leave him and join her on the red team. Gant's death does seem to have jump-started Carter's character: we're finally seeing him respond to Benton's antagonism with something other than resignation, and it's good to see the bit of bad attitude Carter

MOSHE SHAI / SHOOTING STAR

possesses being put to good use. But his decision to ditch Benton is really the only high point in a strangely blasé episode. Even Carol's suspension, following her decision to go to the newspaper with the full story of the patient she accidentally killed, doesn't do much to lift the program out of its doldrums.

"Whose Appy Now?"

Season 3, Episode 14

ORIGINAL AIR DATE: February 6, 1997
WRITTEN BY: Neal Baer
DIRECTED BY: Felix Enriquez Alcalá
GRADE: B+

After what seems like ages, Doug is finally given some meaningful screen time as he treats a teenage cystic-fibrosis patient. The boy, Jad, is just shy of being old enough to authorize his own do-not-resuscitate order, and relies on Doug to convince his mother to take him off the respirator. Doug succeeds at first, but Jad's mother and girlfriend demand that he be intubated again when he stops breathing, leaving Doug frustrated with himself for not being able to follow through with Jad's wishes. This is a smart move by the writers. Instead of embroiling Doug in a confrontation with the boy's mother or the hospital administration over the ethics of the case, they allow him to struggle with himself for a change, which may indicate that recent events in his life have indeed made him more introspective. Clooney hits all the right notes in his performance.

The rest of the episode is given over to humor, all of which works wonderfully as a counterpoint to Doug's frustration. First there's Mark, who, with his new gung-ho dating philosophy, tries to juggle dates with three women on the same day only to have it blow up in his face when they all converge upon him at the same time. It looks very much like he's being prepped to return to a more reserved romantic style after a few weeks of post-Susan shenanigans. Meanwhile, the tension between newly partnered Carter and Maggie (who, much to Carter's dismay, reveals that she's a lesbian), and Benton's anxiety about Carla's pregnancy, are cleverly resolved when Benton is wheeled in for an appendectomy. The procedure is performed by Carter, who revels in his good fortune and snaps photos of his sedated antagonist, who has hallucinations about Hicks, Carter, and Weaver being the mother of his child. It sounds a little over-the-top, but it works quite well somehow. A spoonful of sugar helps the medicine go down, and there's nothing like a little appendectomy humor to keep things from getting too serious.

"The Long Way Around"

Season 3, Episode 15

ORIGINAL AIR DATE: February 13, 1997
WRITTEN BY: Lydia Woodward
DIRECTED BY: Christopher Chulack
GRADE: B

This is a good episode, but a difficult one to judge because of its striking similarity to a very recent episode of *Chicago Hope*, which not only scooped ER on this story line, but also turned out a stronger piece of work in the process. In ER's version of the story, Carol is trapped in a corner store after a botched robbery attempt turns bloody. She, of course, is left to treat the wounded and try to keep the criminals from popping holes in anybody else while they plot their next move. It's unfair, really, to compare this story to *Chicago Hope*'s, but it's impossible not to. On the one hand, this episode's strength is its rare focus on a single character, and Julianna Margulies does an outstanding job of guiding Carol's character through the split-second adaptations to her circumstances that are necessary for her survival. On the other hand, because she's isolated from ER's other characters here, we miss the sense of concern, of a community holding its breath while it prays for its colleague's well-being, that played such an important part in the *Chicago Hope* episode. And although the writers do their best to create an atmosphere of intrigue as Carol tries to figure a way out of her mess, her emotional attachment to one of the shooters, Duncan (played by *Trainspotting*'s Ewan MacGregor), gets in the way of the level of excitement that *Chicago Hope* was able to achieve.

"Faith"

Season 3, Episode 16

ORIGINAL AIR DATE: February 20, 1997
WRITTEN BY: John Wells
DIRECTED BY: Jonathan Kaplan
GRADE: C

Did somebody on ER's staff forget to draw a big red circle around these past few weeks on the production schedule? While the rest of network television has been pulling out all the stops to attract the crucial February sweeps audience, ER has slipped out of gear, plodding along at an uncharacteristically slow pace. This time last season Susan was in the midst of trying to adopt little Susie, Doug was going at his father with all the venom he could muster, and Shep was keeping vigil over his horribly burned partner, Raul ("The Healers"). This week's episode — brace yourself — is really quite boring by comparison. But perhaps this is to be expected when a program whose real dramatic momentum is supplied almost entirely by its characters allows those characters to grope awkwardly through their profound funks. Take Benton, for instance. Yes, his admission to Hicks that he feels some responsibility for Gant's death is an important moment in the development of his character. But his erratic behavior over the past few weeks — at work and with Carla — had already expressed his feelings of guilt far better than he could ever do himself in words, and his revelation to Hicks is therefore downright anticlimactic. The same might be said of Doug's latest run-in with Jad, the cystic-fibrosis patient who'd angrily insisted he be granted a do-not-resuscitate order ("Whose Appy Now?"). The boy has finally turned 18 and ordered Doug to remove him from the respirator so he can die in the presence of his girlfriend. But when Doug removes the tube, Jad struggles briefly and begins to breathe on his own. He checks out and his story peters out, contributing to this week's "not-with-a-bang-but-a-whimper" philosophy.

Of the episode's numerous attempts to construct a compelling story, which include Mark's and Maggie's attempts to place a 35-year-old Down's syndrome patient on a list for a heart transplant, Carter's spot-on diagnosis of a woman in need of an embolectomy whose problems Anspaugh hastily attributes to digestive discomfort, and Jeanie's ongoing "should I or shouldn't I" torment about becoming intimate with Greg Fischer, it's Carol's argument with her mother about her motivation for studying to become a doctor that pays the biggest dividends. Aside from shedding some useful light on her relationship with her mother, the spat also demonstrates Carol's own ambivalence about her decision to alter her career path. Most important, it's a rare moment of energy in what is otherwise a near-comatose episode.

"Tribes"

Season 3, Episode 17

ORIGINAL AIR DATE: April 10, 1997
WRITTEN BY: Lance Gentile
DIRECTED BY: Richard Thorpe
GRADE: A-

It's not exactly a banner day for race relations at Cook County, but the tension produced by Mark's apparent prejudice toward patients of color does, at long last, put a little buzz back into the show. Sure, it's odd that we're suddenly seeing a side of Mark we've never seen before, but why take the air out of a show that's finally pumped itself up after a few weeks of deflated and misshapen story lines? Certain that an elderly black woman complaining of chest pains is just another crack addict, Mark pawns her off on Carter, who discovers that she suffers from serious heart problems that another hospital, dismissing her much the way Mark does, has missed. In the episode's central story, Mark assumes that a black teen who's been shot is a gang member, only to find he was an innocent bystander at the shooting and is a local basketball hero. Although Mark's recurrent confrontations with the boy's brother, Chris, create the charged atmosphere necessary to the exploration of the charged issue of race relations, it's actually his inner struggle to understand the basis of his assumptions, manifested in his awkward attempts to placate Malik and Haleh, that makes this episode satisfyingly unsettling. Some will find that this story plays the "race card" too bluntly, but it's a winner nonetheless.

It's also refreshing to see Benton starting to pull himself back together. He smilingly accepts a spot on Hicks's surgical team and marvels at Carla's ultrasound in an ultra-fatherly way after she's brought in following a traffic accident. He even catches a break when Jeanie, classy as always, puts aside her past relationship with him and treats Carla with respect and sensitivity. With any luck, Jeanie's newfound self-assuredness will lead to some kind of resolution of her ever-incipient relationship with Greg. For some reason, the writers have tried to use the Jeanie-Greg romantic story to string us along just as they used to do with Susan and Mark. It isn't working. Jeanie has to be allowed to make a decision before Greg — and, more importantly, the viewing public — lose interest.

"You Bet Your Life"

Season 3, Episode 18

ORIGINAL AIR DATE: April 17, 1997
WRITTEN BY: Paul Manning
DIRECTED BY: Christopher Chulack
GRADE: B+

The latest in a series of middle-of-the-road episodes proves two things. First, that ER has a maddening tendency lately to move its character studies along in quick jerks that somehow lead nowhere fast. Second, that despite this the show is still probably the best thing on television, weakened only by its inability to maintain its impossibly high narrative standard for an entire season.

Jeanie has what may or may not be a breakthrough moment when she lashes out at Greg for refusing to comfort a blind AIDS patient and then, moved by the experience, goes to Al Boulet to clear her conscience. It could be that she's had it with Greg. It could be that she's interested in saving her marriage with Al. It could be that she's just taken another turn in the eternal waffling to which her character has been consigned since she first landed on the show. Meanwhile, Carol's showing no signs of climbing out of the rut of her med-school angst. And although the story of Mark's treatment of a woman who swallows an entire tray of surgical instruments is amusing, it turns into yet another tale of Weaver's one-up-doctorship of poor, pathetic Mark Greene. Thank heavens Benton's finally being cut some slack by Carla and the show's writers. Perhaps this story will make some much-needed progress now that she's allowing him to take part in her pregnancy. It also appears that Carter's being thrown back into the mix. His decision to override Anspaugh's refusal to grant surgery to a dying man by tricking Hicks into scrubbing in with him makes for some exciting television — especially when Hicks places him on probation and tells him she'd lobbied to have him kicked out entirely. What's more, it suggests that the best remedy for the administrative ruthlessness Carter's been crusading against for three years may, in fact, be a little ruthlessness of his own. This story is only mildly hampered by the utter impossibility of Carter's being let go, which would turn off a large chunk of those 18-to-40-year-old female viewers. Praise the lord and pass me that chart of key demographics.

"Calling Dr. Hathaway"

Season 3, Episode 19

ORIGINAL AIR DATE: April 24, 1997
WRITTEN BY: Samantha Howard Corbin and Jason Cahill (teleplay)
    and Neal Baer (story)
DIRECTED BY: Paris Barclay
GRADE: B+

Only on ER could three writers exercise their collective courage and creative will in order to depict the event that may mark Benton's most profound character development to date: grocery shopping. It might not sound like "must-see TV," but it works. We've become so accustomed to Benton's blustering attempts to solve his problems through confrontation that his simple resignation to his role in Carla's pregnancy catches us pleasantly off-guard. Instead of throwing himself into his work — his usual reaction to whatever trouble comes his way — he takes the day off to help Carla out. The significance of his efforts doesn't escape his sister, and he manages not to come off as the embarrassingly proud and predictable father-to-be. Oh, sure, he's as crusty as ever, but he seems finally to have been allowed to get off the roller coaster that the writers have kept him on for most of the season. His character has at last reached a satisfying equilibrium. With any luck, he'll be allowed to explore this brave new world of contentment for a while longer.

Carter also seems to have reached a moment of truth himself. All of the various parts of his character that we've glimpsed in varying degrees for the past three seasons — the innocence, the attitude, the responsibility, the goofiness, et cetera — are coalescing. He demonstrated this last week in outmaneuvering Anspaugh, and keeps it up when he calls Edson on failing to take a full history of a patient and then covering his tracks afterward. Carter's always been an interesting character, but a strangely weak one too. Now he's coming into his own, and his newfound maturity is breathing some new life into the show. The same can't be said for Carol, who, despite doing great on her MCAT, still isn't sure whether she's MD material. It's about time that Julianna Margulies was given something better to do with her character.

"Random Acts"

Season 3, Episode 20

ORIGINAL AIR DATE: May 1, 1997
WRITTEN BY: Carol Flint
DIRECTED BY: Jonathan Kaplan
GRADE: A-

After lurching through the prime-time schedule without much sense of direction for pretty much the whole season, ER has broken into its sprint for the finish of season three. All its viewers can do is try to keep up. This week's big event, of course, is the sudden and violent beating Mark receives in a hospital washroom. The raw energy of this scene is emphasized by some wonderfully manic camera work, and the footage of Mark lying prone on the floor while the sounds and shadows of his co-workers filter through the closed bathroom door captures his disorientation fantastically. Although we're left to wonder who Mark's attacker is, the larger question is how the incident will affect his performance in the ER.

While this turn of events leaps off the screen, the rest of the episode is rather more subdued — but nonetheless effective. Although it's not quite as ballistic, Jeanie's sudden shying away from Greg and warming up to Al is at least as significant a moment. Now that her character has taken some tentative steps toward living her life instead of surviving her disease, the time seems right for her to focus on Al instead of his HIV. Although some viewers will, like Weaver at first, find Jeanie's renewed interest in Al hard to stomach, the writers seem poised to take the bold step of reuniting the couple in order to broaden their dramatization of AIDS in society. They, like Jeanie herself, are taking a big risk, but might just produce some groundbreaking television as a result.

The decision to have Benton and Carter team up again is also a good one. Benton's serious (as opposed to annoyed) puzzlement at Carter's decision to leave a big-name debriefing in order to talk to a patient is another sign that his relationship with Carla is giving him pause to reflect not only on his personal life, but on his professional one as well. Ironically, the writers have rejuvenated Benton's up-in-the-air character by injecting it with a healthy dose of ambivalence. Now if they could only find some way to work Doug back into a meaningful story line.

"Make a Wish"

Season 3, Episode 21

ORIGINAL AIR DATE: May 8, 1997
WRITTEN BY: Lydia Woodward (teleplay) and Joe Sachs (story)
DIRECTED BY: Richard Thorpe
GRADE: B+

A large segment of ER's viewership is probably waiting for Benton to return to his take-charge ways, and may even find the writer's decision just to let things *happen* to him a trifle frustrating. This episode addresses that frustration by showing that it's Benton's own, and that even his most frantic attempts to act are futile given the circumstances into which he's been inserted. His pestering of the doctors during Carla's premature delivery, which he later admits was a manifestation of his fear, is a concrete example of what we've suspected about Benton all along: a lot of his bombastic action up to now has actually been *re*action to the hand life has dealt him. The only difference now is that he seems finally to have realized this himself. This marks a significant moment in the development of his character and opens the door for Eriq La Salle to present a more consistently nuanced character.

In contrast, nothing about Mark's return to the ER after his beating suggests that his character will be covering new ground. Sure, he may be shaken up for a few weeks, but we've followed him down this path before and know that he usually ends up right back where he started. Now if he were to take Maggie up on her offer of armament and blow somebody away, that would certainly give his character a good, hard twist, but he's more likely to be hit by a falling Russian spy satellite. And just when Carol resolves her career crisis, Carter flings himself into one by asking about switching from surgery to emergency

medicine. Different characters, same old story. And given the fact that
Carol's vocational angst — like bombshell pediatrician Anna Del
Amico's sudden appearance — is looking more and more as though
it was designed to distract us from the possibility of a long-awaited
reunion with Doug, it's easy to be suspicious of the writers' motives
for tossing Carter into professional limbo. But since next week is the
season finale, who can tell what will happen?

"One More for the Road"

Season 3, Episode 22

ORIGINAL AIR DATE: May 15, 1997
WRITTEN BY: John Wells
DIRECTED BY: Christopher Chulack
GRADE: A

This episode does just what a season finale should do. It leaves some
issues open, resolves others, and allows just enough room for the
writers to turn the tables on us come next season. The story that
seems most likely to have been resolved is Carter's. The tension
between him and Anspaugh after Carter announces his desire to
switch from surgery back to the emergency room is incredible, and
Noah Wyle and John Aylward turn in perhaps their best performances
of the year. The issue now isn't so much whether Carter will be
allowed to return to the ER, but whether Anspaugh's character will
just fade away now that he can no longer play Carter's chief antagonist. It's a safe bet that the viewing public is hoping for as thoroughly
satisfying a resolution of Doug and Carol's story, and wants all the
passion of that long, warm kiss to still be around come next season.
But given ER's tendency to perform narrative procedures in the dark
— having things happen over the summer that we never get to see —
it's probably best to expect the unexpected as far as Doug and Carol
go. The wonder of it all is that, having held out this long, and having
allowed Susan to float out of Mark's life earlier in the season, the
writers have decided, however briefly, to end the tease and give
viewers what they want.

We'll have to wait until next year to see how Benton is settling into
parenthood (assuming the baby survives a long, hot Chicago summer) and whether Mark continues to be haunted by his beating
(which did, at least, afford the writers the opportunity this week to
exploit his resemblance to Bernard Goetz). And who knows what
state Jeanie and Al's relationship, let alone their health, will be in
when next we see them? It's been a season of spotty quality. Let's
hope that mulling over what they've left themselves during the hiatus
puts some wind in the writers' sails for next season.

In the '60s, TV gave us cute caring doctors like Ben Casey and Dr. Kildare. In the '70s, Marcus Welby M.D., kind and fatherly. And in the '80s, it was the wacky but lovable gang at St. Elsewhere. But this is the '90s. Health care reform is dead. And nowhere is it deader than on NBC's new hospital drama. In this medical zoo, patients check in sick and they leave the place...

I'm **Doctor Mark Scream!** I'm very **good** at **yelling** out **orders** to **help** keep this **hectic**, understaffed **hospital going!** I'll **show** you what I **mean!** *Put the* **kid** *who* **stopped** *a* **shotgun** *blast with his* **chest** *in Trauma* **One!** *Put the* *guy who had a* **fight** *with a* **pit bull** *in Trauma* **Two!** *Put the* **pit bull** *in Trauma* **Three!** *Put up* *new* **wallpaper** *in O.R. 7! And get me an* **ear** **specialist!** *I think I just* **blew** *out an* **eardrum** *from* **listening** *to myself* **shout** *so much!*

I'm **Doctor Loss**, the beefcake pediatrician! I not only **deliver babies**, I personally **help** as many **women** as I can **conceive** them! My **bedside manner** includes getting in bed with **E.R.** patients! And, if it's a **slow** day, well, there's always the **nurses**, the **aides**, the ladies who **work** in the hospital cafeteria and that **cute pit bull** in Trauma Three!

I'm **Doctor Lose-It**, my **specialty** is **delving** into the **emotional** side of a patient's **problems!** Don't be **fooled** by my **monotone delivery** and **good looks!** I've had **extensive** experience **dealing** with **thieving, self-destructive, psycho** types — mainly me and my **wacko sister!**

WE HAVE A WHEEZER!

MUMMY DEAREST

MVA COMING THROUGH!

KERVOR-KIAN

NYPD ADIEU

25¢ 10 MINUTE 50¢ ?

NINTENDO

Every **two minutes** they wheel another **emergency victim** through those **doors!** Is the **hospital** always this **busy?**

Not really! When there are **no emergencies**, we **wheel** the **same** patient **in** and **out!** It makes us **look busy** so the people in the **waiting room** don't get **antsy!**

What did that **huge** guy **Jerky** do **before** he **worked** here?

He **worked overseas!** He **was part** of the **Berlin Wall!**

4

THE
AUTHORITATIVE
ER
DRINKING
GAME

If you're one of the millions of viewers who sit through
NBC's entire Thursday night lineup waiting for ER, chances
are you're ready for a good, stiff drink by 10:00 P.M. Let's
face it — *Suddenly Susan* has probably driven more people
to drink than a limo service on prom night. So why not
grab the beverage of your choice, familiarize yourself
with the rules of the game, and strap yourself in for an
hour of self-medication?

It's important to remember, of course, that whether
you're drinking to avoid your problems, to forget (that
Brooke Shields has her own prime-time series), or just to
have fun, the rapid consumption of alcohol can have serious effects. Doug Ross himself would be quick to offer the
following caution.

Even when taken in smaller amounts than we've seen
Doug put back after a tough day at work, alcohol can
impair judgment and motor skills. It can also lead to
slurred speech and a sense of euphoria, which, when
experienced in combination, can be embarrassing at best
and dangerous at worst. Increased alcohol intake can lead
to hypoglycemia (low blood sugar) and, if drunk to the

extent that one's blood alcohol concentration (BAC) is raised to between 0.30 and 0.50 BAC, can cause unconsciousness and respiratory depression. The common term for this condition is "alcohol poisoning," and it doesn't take a brain surgeon, or even a reasonable television facsimile thereof (see Adam Arkin on *Chicago Hope*), to figure out what the "toxic" in "intoxication" stands for. In extreme cases (usually a BAC of around 0.50), death may occur, usually after victims pass out and their stomach contents end up in their lungs. This is sometimes referred to by the medical term "drowning in your own vomit."

Were Doug to encounter you in such a state in a *real* ER, you can be sure he wouldn't waste his time tousling your hair and calling you "little buddy." He'd be more likely to bark an order for physostigmine 0.02-0.06 mg/kg IV or IM, or, if you've suffered massive keto-acidosis, to order therapy with Nabic, glucose 5-10%, and possibly a Lasix IV.

Then again, if Doug were to join you in your living room for a little Thursday-night revelry, he'd probably be yelling "Beer — stat!" louder than anyone else. You pays your money and you takes your chances. But remember: You wouldn't watch ER and drive, so don't drink and drive either.

THE GAME

Warm-up: If anyone in the room has not seen a commercial proclaiming this week's episode to be "the one ER you absolutely must not miss," take a drink. If a voice-over announcement to this effect is made during the closing credits of *Suddenly Susan*, chug. Now you're ready to begin.

1. Take a *small sip* (less than a mouthful) every time:
   • a doctor lets fly with an incomprehensible string of abbreviations

- someone says "stat"
- a firefighter, police officer, or paramedic shows up
- someone shows up in weird or inappropriate clothing
- someone says "multiple gunshot wounds"
- someone sleeps with someone he or she shouldn't
- someone complains about not getting enough sleep
- the defibrillator is used (one sip for each time "clear!" is yelled)
- comic relief is provided by a patient admitted under the influence of a drug
- doctors work out problems on the basketball court
- sexual tension between Mark and Susan is obvious to everyone but them
- the gang heads to Magoo's for a nice, greasy meal
- Peter Benton acts like a jerk
- John Carter is taught a new procedure
- Carter does something stupid or brilliant
- Carter encounters an attractive young female patient
- Carter competes with another student
- Mark Greene tries to leave the ER but is held up by an emergency
- Mark misses or forgets an appointment because he's too busy in the ER
- Mark reluctantly exercises his authority
- Carol Hathaway offers sensitive counsel to an anxious patient
- Carol looks at Doug when he's not looking
- Susan Lewis argues with another doctor
- Susan has to cover for Chloe
- Doug Ross tousles a child's hair and/or calls him or her "little buddy," "kiddo," etc.
- Doug lectures a parent on his/her parenting skills; twice if he calls Social Services
- Doug gives Carol that "lost puppy" look
- Doug makes an advance toward Carol and is rejected
- Doug has casual sex; twice if it's with a stewardess
- Kerry Weaver rubs somebody the wrong way

2. **Take a drink (a pleasing mouthful) every time:**
   - someone is intubated
   - someone says "gastric lavage"
   - someone calls security
   - a member of the staff complains about managed-care programs or demands to treat a patient who has no insurance
   - someone complains about the inept treatment given at another hospital
   - trauma occurs without musical accompaniment
   - a scene is shot in the hospital cafeteria
   - Benton says something nice
   - Benton screws up a procedure
   - Benton smiles; twice if he laughs
   - Benton fulfills a familial responsibility
   - John Carter is called something other than "Carter"
   - Carter is taught a new procedure, and Benton isn't the instructor
   - Carter gets a procedure right the first time
   - Carter does something stupid that turns out to be brilliant
   - Mark fights with Doug
   - Mark tries to make his marriage work
   - Mark scores with someone other than his wife
   - Mark isn't wearing scrubs
   - Doug takes a drink
   - Doug kisses Carol
   - Doug has casual sex with a hospital employee
   - Doug questions someone's authority
   - Susan wins an argument with another doctor
   - Susan shows up in her black dress
   - Susan kisses a fellow staff member
   - Weaver is compassionate

3. **Chug (finish your drink without hesitation or, at very least, before the next commercial break) every time:**
   - an episode follows a single plot

- a firefighter, police officer, and paramedic are in the room at the same time
- you make the diagnosis before the ER staff does
- a member of the ER staff, or immediate family, is admitted as a patient
- Benton compliments Carter
- Carter explains why he's still in the ER
- Mark and Susan admit their love for one another
- Mark goes an entire episode without getting that concerned look on his face
- Carol attempts suicide
- Doug rejects a woman's advances
- Doug sleeps with Carol
- Weaver jokes about her disability

D
R
I
N
K
I
N
G

G
A
M
E

4. **Apply alcohol intravenously if:**
   - Benton reveals that he's never actually been to medical school
   - Carter tells Benton to fuck off
   - Mark is arrested for child molestation
   - Carol dies
   - Susan admits that the reason she's so tired is that she's moonlighting as a stripper
   - Doug comes out of the closet
   - Weaver blames her attitude on PMS
   - a doctor refers a patient to Chicago Hope

GEORGE CLOONEY FILMOGRAPHY

RETURN TO HORROR HIGH (1987)

PRODUCER: Mark Lisson
DIRECTOR: Bill Froelich
SCREENPLAY: Bill Froelich, Mark Lisson, Dana
  Escalante, Greg H. Sims
CAST: Vince Edwards, Brendan Hughes, Scott Jacoby,
  Lori Lethin, Philip McKeon, Alex Rocco

This turkey didn't exactly rocket Clooney to stardom, and
it's little wonder. He plays a throwaway character named
Oliver in this chase-and-slash movie about a group of
filmmakers who go to a high school where a number
of grisly murders took place. Unfortunately, they're not
alone, and a killer stalks the filmmakers and picks them
off one by one.

RETURN OF THE KILLER TOMATOES! (1988)

PRODUCER: J. Stephen Peace
DIRECTOR: John De Bello

SCREENPLAY: Constantine Dillon, J. Stephen Peace, and John De Bello

CAST: John Astin, Karen Mistal, Anthony Starke

Every expense is spared in this sequel to the infamously bad *Attack of the Killer Tomatoes*, in which the demented Professor Gangreen finds a way to transform tomatoes into beefcake humans through a combination of gene splicing and rock music. Mixed among the hokey footage of giant tomatoes and lame sight gags are some truly funny moments — a vengeful mob descends upon a fuzzy tomato named F.T., and a fight breaks out between cowboys and ninjas for no apparent reason — but the movie is generally content just to revel in its own schlock. Clooney looks alternately bemused and uninterested as Matt Stevens, a pizza cook and the best friend of the movie's hero, but he does land the best deadpan line of the movie: "That was the bravest thing I've ever seen a vegetable do."

RED SURF (1990)

PRODUCER: Richard C. Weinman

DIRECTOR: H. Gordon Boos

SCREENPLAY: Vincent Robert

CAST: Philip McKeon, Dedee Pfeiffer, Doug Savant, Gene Simmons

Clooney stars as Mark Remar in this so-so action flick about two drug-dealing surfer dudes who decide to get out of the business after one last score. They run into trouble when one of their friends turns out to be an informer and sets them up for a big fall. Not a cinematic pièce de résistance, but worth a look just to see Clooney's Big Sur hairdo.

THE HARVEST (1992)

PRODUCERS: Jason Clark, David A. Jackson, Morgan
  Mason, Carole Curb Nemoy
DIRECTOR: David Marconi
SCREENPLAY: David Marconi and John Rice
CAST: Anthony Denison, Miguel Ferrer, Harvey Fierst-
  ein, Leilani Sarelle, Henry Silva

Ferrer, Clooney's cousin, plays a screenwriter who is
drugged and has his kidney stolen for sale on the human-
organ black market while he's investigating a series of
murders in Mexico. Sound familiar? The screenplay is
based on a popular urban legend. Don't blink, or you'll
miss Clooney in his very brief cameo as a gaudily made-
up, lip-synching transvestite who struts his/her stuff in a
seedy club to the tune of "Heaven Is a Place on Earth."
On second thought, maybe it's best just to blink and try
to pretend you didn't see Clooney shake his stuff in this
particular way.

FROM DUSK TILL DAWN (1996)

PRODUCERS: Gianni Nunnari and Meir Teper
DIRECTOR: Robert Rodriguez
SCREENPLAY: Quentin Tarantino
CAST: Salma Hayek, Harvey Keitel, Juliette Lewis,
  Ernest Lui, Richard "Cheech" Marin, Tom Savini,
  Quentin Tarantino, Fred Williamson

Clooney and Tarantino star as brothers Seth and Richie
Gecko, two small-time hoods who shoot their way out of
a Texan bank heist and cross the border into Mexico with
the unwilling assistance of Jacob Fuller (Keitel) and his
children. The story takes a wild turn from road movie to
splatterfest when the Fullers' motor home pulls into a

Mexico roadhouse which just happens to be infested with vampires. Clooney is great as the tattooed, gun-toting nasty, and the movie, though not hilarious, has a comic, campy charm that all the blood can't obscure.

ONE FINE DAY (1996)

PRODUCER: Lydia Obst
DIRECTOR: Michael Hoffman
SCREENPLAY: Terrell Selter and Ellen Simon
CAST: Charles Durning, Ellen Greene, Robert Klein, Alex D. Linz, Michelle Pfeiffer, Mae Whitman

Jack Taylor (Clooney) and Melanie Parker (Pfeiffer) are two hardworking, divorced parents who meet on the worst day of their respective lives and somehow manage to make things even worse. This is a romantic comedy, so of course they hate each other immediately. And of course this means that it's really a case of love at first sight. And of course both of them are too stubborn to admit their

One Fine Day
FOX / SHOOTING STAR

feelings. And of course they end up in each other's arms by the end of the day. But it's a charming movie with some genuinely funny moments, most of them provided by Melanie's son, Sammy (Linz), who steals every scene he's in.

BATMAN AND ROBIN (1997)

PRODUCER: Peter MacGregor-Scott
DIRECTOR: Joel Schumacher
SCREENPLAY: Akiva Goldsman and
    Christopher McQuarrie
CAST: Elle Macpherson, Chris O'Donnell, Arnold
    Schwarzenegger, Alicia Silverstone, Uma Thurman

Clooney does his best as the caped crusader, but this film is more interested in its look than in any of its characters. Batman teams up with Robin and new addition Batgirl (Silverstone) to face the evil Poison Ivy (Thurman) and foil Mr. Freeze (Schwarzenegger) in his attempts to turn Gotham City into his personal snow globe, and the punches and punchlines fly fast and furious in Schumacher's campy take on the Batman franchise. You'll like this one a whole lot more if you fast-forward through the dialogue and just sit back and admire the incredible sets and cinematography on a big-screen TV.

THE PEACEMAKER (1997)

PRODUCER: Branko Lustig
DIRECTOR: Mimi Leder
SCREENPLAY: Michael Schiffer
CAST: Michael Boatman, Joan Copeland, Carlos Gomez,
    Nicole Kidman, Holt McCallany, Armin Mueller-
    Stahl, Gary Wentz

Clooney, the peacemaker

SCOTT R. SUTTON / ARCHIVE PHOTOS

Mimi Leder, the acclaimed director from ER, takes the helm of the first picture from the new DreamWorks SKG studio, which is headed by entertainment moguls Steven Spielberg, Jeffrey Katzenberg, and David Geffen. Clooney plays a no-nonsense American colonel who teams up with Kidman to stop a maniac who has stolen a nuclear warhead and is threatening to detonate it in Manhattan. It's a stylish action-thriller in which Clooney finally, 10 years after his first film, proves that he is a movie star.

HARRY LANGDON / SHOOTING STAR

CLOONEYISMS

"Children with hives are not cute."

★

"It's not the first time I've been clawed by an angry female."

★

"Women do not respond well to men who come on to them while wearing wedding rings."

★

"You don't invite somebody to Hawaii to play Scrabble by the pool."

★

KAREN: "I'll reward you when we get back."
DOUG: "Let's go back."

★

MARK: "Does this mean you and Linda are that serious?"
DOUG: "Serious? Our longest phone conversation is 'Get over here.'"

★

MARK: "What do *you* know about penance?"
DOUG: "I dated a lot of Catholic girls."

★

CAROL: "Where'd you find her, Doug?"
DOUG: "My house."
CAROL: "What's her name?"
DOUG: "I don't know."

★

"I promise not to pass along any misogyny with the basketball tips."

★

MARK: "Do I detect a lack of enthusiasm?"

DOUG: "Beats putting in chest tubes."

*

MARK: "You can't take the fact that I'm your boss."

DOUG: "That's typically narcissistic of you, Mark. I can't take the fact that anyone is my boss."

*

MARK: "Go ahead and say it. I'm a sanctimonious, judgmental, self-righteous, sexually frustrated little man."

DOUG: "Well, you're not little."

*

"All right, get this. There are two brownies in the fridge. They aren't birthday cake, and they aren't mine, but I think we should steal them."

*

BENTON: "One, two . . ."

DOUG: ". . . buckle my shoe. And kiss my ass."

*

HARPER: "How do you handle the stress?"

DOUG: "I tend to drink, but I'm not the best role model."

*

MARK: "Don't do it, Doug. It's a big mistake."

DOUG: "Well, you know what my father always said: 'If you're gonna make a mistake, make it a big one.'"

*

CAROL: "Doug, you promised me you wouldn't tell anybody about my birthday."

DOUG: "That was last year."

CAROL: "Yeah, and you told everybody then, too."

DOUG: "At least I'm consistent."

*

E-RAY: "Dr. Ross, it's your father again."

DOUG: "Tell him I died — beautiful funeral, everybody cried."

*

SUSAN: "Carter's been hanging around Benton too much."

DOUG: "Haven't we all."

*

DOUG: "I never cared for her. Unsupporting and controling and manipulative. You want me to go on with this?"

MARK: "Yeah, please. I'm enjoying it."

DOUG: "Demanding, skinny legs."

MARK: "What are you doing looking at my wife's legs?"

DOUG: "I'm your buddy, I'm not dead."

*

"Does it come as a big shock to you that I was intimate with someone who I am less than soul mates with?"

*

"Do me a favor. Don't come to me for tips on women anymore. If I choose to have a Roman orgy with farm animals in my free time, that is none of your business. That is none of anyone's business."

*

DOUG: "There is an ugly, vicious rumor going around that Kerry Weaver . . ."

MARK: "Don't start with me."

DOUG: "So it's true."

MARK: "I don't know what everyone is so upset about. Kerry Weaver isn't that bad."

DOUG: "She's great."

MARK: "She grows on you."

DOUG: "Been hitting the Prozac again?"

*

". . . starring Weaver and the sound of her own voice: a love story."

*

CAROL: "You okay?"

DOUG: "Well, generally, this has not been a good day. Specifically, this has not been a good day."

*

CAROL: "I have no reason to ever question your integrity."

DOUG: "Not as a doctor, at least."

*

CAROL: "You can smell snow coming — it has a smell."

DOUG: "Smells like burritos."

*

"I'm not a grown-up doctor."

★

CAROL: "She can get through medical school, and I can't even get through the door."

DOUG: "You can get through *my* door."

★

"You're eating hospital food? You're that desperate? Come on, let's get some lunch."

★

PATIENT: "Why are you taking a picture of my head when my leg hurts?"

DOUG: "Because I'm the doctor and that's what I want to do."

★

"Looks like our next lucky contestant has arrived."

★

"Anybody have X-ray vision? No? Well, then, we'll have to get radiology to look at it."

★

HALEH: "What happened to his brain tumor?"

DOUG: "It was cured when he was struck by lightning."

★

"Page me if you need me. And by the way, Carter, you *do* need me."

★

MARK: "Remember when we were going to save the world?"

DOUG: "Nah, I was always in it for the money."

★

JERRY: "We got a marriage proposal on the fax."

DOUG: "Does it include a bank statement?"

★

"My New Year's resolution is to avoid charitable impulses."

★

MARK: "What do you think? Chop House for Valentine's Day?"

DOUG: "Mark, I'd love to, but you're not my type."

★

"Are you dating a patient? Do the words 'Exxon Valdez' mean anything to you?"

   ★

"Thank you, Carol. Point out something else I know nothing about."

   ★

MARK: "I thought I'd get her a puppy for Christmas."

DOUG: "In case you haven't noticed, that dog's like eight years old. It's ready for a midlife crisis. It's ready for fur replacement."

   ★

FRIEND: "So, white men *can* jump."

DOUG: "Yeah, but they can't land."

   ★

MARK: "I used to think of this as a family. Didn't it feel like that?"

DOUG: "Yeah, well, you've got to remember my idea of family is a little screwed up."

   ★

"Ladies and gentlemen, thank you all very much for this tremendous honor. I want to take this opportunity to acknowledge some of my colleagues. First, David Morgenstern for his stalwart support. One minute he's stamping my walking papers, and the next he has his face so far up my butt if he had a mustache it would tickle my throat. Let's not forget Neil Bernstein. Neil: proof that any idiot who can nod his head can rise right to the middle of pediatric medicine. And last, but definitely not least, Mark Greene. Mark 'the self-righteous shall inherit the ER' Greene. Mark 'I am behind you 110 percent, but you are outta here' Greene. Thank-you. Kiss my ass. Good night. God bless."

WORKS
CONSULTED

Cawley, Janet. "George Clooney: Facing Fame with His Feet on the Ground." *Biography* Aug. 1997: 26–31.

Clooney, George. Interview with Cynthia McFadden. "Clooney Unmasked." *Prime Time Live.* ABC. 14 May 1997.

———. Interview by Carrie Fisher. "George Clooney's Declaration of Independence." *George* June 1997: 88–91, 110–11.

———. Interview. *Mr. Showbiz Interview.* 20 Dec. 1996. Online. 11 July 1997.

———. Interview with Oprah Winfrey. *Oprah Winfrey.* Harpo Productions. 20 June 1997.

———. Interview by Ian Dwight. "The *Tribute* Interview: George Clooney." *Tribute* June 1997: 30–32.

Clooney, Rosemary. Interview with Tom Snyder. *Late Late Show.* CBS. 15 July 1997.

Daley, Steve. "Boy George!" *Entertainment Weekly.* 26 Jan. 1996. *Entertainment Weekly Online.* Online.

"Dance Fever." *People. People Cover Story Online.* Online.

"ER." *NBC.com.* 1997. Online.

"ER Staff Joins George Clooney's ET Boycott." *Mr. Showbiz News.* 31 Oct. 1996. Online.

Errico, Marcus. "Clooney Amputates ET." *E! Online.* 28 Oct. 1996. Online.

———. "Now Superman Won't Talk to ET Either." *E! Online.* 31 Oct. 1996. Online.

Feran, Tim. "Nick Clooney Enjoying Success as AMC's Host,

George's Dad." *Columbus Dispatch* 16 Apr. 1996. *The News-Times Online*. Online.

Fink, Mitchell. "Insider." *People. People Online*. Online.

"George Clooney." *Entertainment Weekly Online*. 1996. Online.

Giammarco, David. "How to Succeed in Show Business by Really Trying." *Globe and Mail* 26 Sept. 1997: E4.

Glieberman, Owen. "Monster Mishmash." *Entertainment Weekly Online*. 2 Feb. 1996. Online.

"Iggy Says: The Pot-Bellied Pig as a Pet." *Columbus Free Press*. Online.

Meyers, Kate. "ER: The Doctors Unmasked." *Entertainment Weekly Online*. 1996. Online.

O'Donnell, Chris. Interview with Jane Wollman Rusoff. *Mr. Showbiz Interview*. 11 Oct. 1996. Online.

Pearlman, Cindy. "Cape Four." *Cinescape* Mar.-Apr. 1997: 18–21.

Pfeiffer, Michelle. Interview with Jane Wollman Rusoff. *Mr. Showbiz Interview*. 19 Dec. 1996. Online.

"Pot Bellied Pig Directory." *AcmePet Exotic Pet Directory*. Online.

Richmond, Peter. "The Keeper of the Flame." *GQ* Oct. 1997: 234–39, 294–95.

Rochlin, Margy. "George Clooney." *Us* July 1997: 50–56, 100.

Rusoff, Jane Wollman. "Better a Hunk than a Schmuck." *Mr. Showbiz Interview*. 20 Dec. 1996. Online.

Schneider, Karen S., Pam Lambert, and Gregory Cerio. "Smooth Operator." *People. People Cover Story Online*. Online.

Schwartz, Mindy. "Bell's Palsy." Mar. 1994. *University Health Services: Topics in Primary Care*. Online.

Schwarzbaum, Lisa. "National Endowment of the Smarts." *Entertainment Weekly* 16 Feb. 1996: 24–25.

"Spielberg Beats *Green Hornet* in Battle for ER Star." *Detroit News* 15 Dec. 1995. *Detroit News Online*. Online.

"Warner Prescribes a $25-Million Deal to Lure Clooney to *Batman*." *Detroit News* 2 Mar. 1996. *Detroit News Online*. Online.

Watson, Bret. "What's Up Docs?" *Entertainment Weekly Online*. 1996. Online.

Wulf, Steve. "Lights, Camera, Reaction." *Time* 13 Nov. 1995. *Pathfinder*. Online.

ACKNOWLEDGMENTS

I am indebted to Stuart Ross for his sharp-eyed editorial work and to Heather Keenleyside for her inspiration and snarky moral support. Thanks also to Stephan Morin for all the laughs and for leading me to the blue hair.